Writing Software Manuals

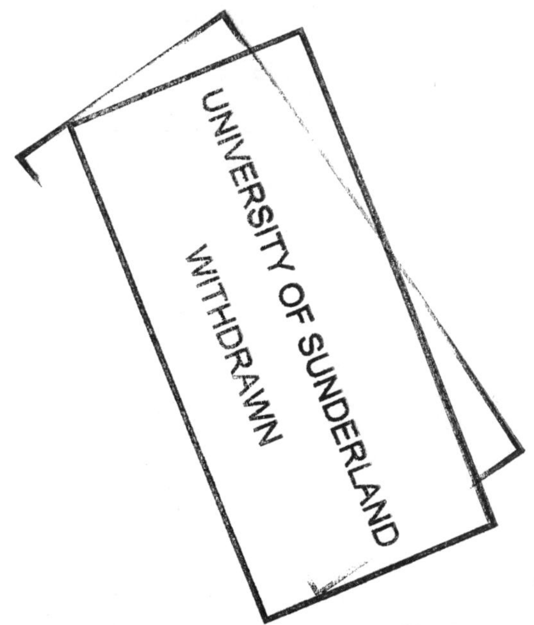

BCS Practitioner Series

Series editor: Ray Welland

Writing Software Manuals

A practical guide

Martyn Thirlway

Prentice Hall

New York   London   Toronto   Sydney   Tokyo   Singapore

First published 1994 by
Prentice Hall International (UK) Ltd
Campus 400, Maylands Avenue
Hemel Hempstead
Hertfordshire, HP2 7EZ
A division of
Simon & Schuster International Group

© Prentice Hall International (UK) Ltd, 1994

Typeset in 10/12 pt Times
by MHL Typesetting Ltd., Coventry

Printed in Great Britain at the University Press, Cambridge

Library of Congress Cataloging-in-Publication Data

Thirlway, Martyn.
  Writing software manuals : a practical guide / Martyn Thirlway.
    p. cm. — (The BCS practitioner series)
  Includes bibliographical references and index.
  ISBN 0-13-138801-0
  1. Electronic data processing documentation. 2. Computer software —
Handbooks, manuals, etc.   I. Title. II. Series.
  QA76.9.D6T49   1994
  808'.066005 — dc20   94-14088
                                                                        CIP

British Library Cataloguing in Publication Data

A catalogue record for this book is available from
the British Library

ISBN 0-13-138801-0

---

1 2 3 4 5 98 97 96 95 94

To my mother, who first awakened my interest in the richness and power of the English language, and to Joanne Hough, without whose love and encouragement this book would never have been written

Contents

Editorial preface

The aim of the BCS Practitioner Series is to produce books that are relevant for practising computer professionals across the whole spectrum of Information Technology activities. We want to encourage practitioners to share their practical experience of methods and applications with fellow professionals. We also seek to disseminate information in a form that is suitable for the practitioner who often has only limited time to read widely within a new subject area or to assimilate research findings.

The role of the BCS is to provide advice on the suitability of books for the Series, via the Editorial Panel, and to provide a pool of potential authors upon which we can draw. Our objective is that this Series will reinforce the drive within the BCS to increase professional standards in IT. The other partners in this venture, Prentice Hall, provide the publishing expertise and international marketing capabilities of a leading publisher in the computing field.

The response when we set up the Series was extremely encouraging. However, the success of the Series depends on there being practitioners who want to learn as well as those who feel they have something to offer! The Series is under continual development and we are always looking for ideas for new topics and feedback on how to further improve the usefulness of the Series. If you are interested in writing for the Series then please contact us.

The quality of documentation has been a source of complaints for as long as I have been involved in computing (and probably long before that too!). Here is a book which gives practical advice on how to construct high-quality manuals. The author has drawn on his extensive experience in technical writing and the book is illustrated with many useful examples. If you are involved in producing software documentation then this will be a useful book.

Ray Welland
Computing Science Department, University of Glasgow

Editorial Panel Members
Frank Bott (UCW, Aberystwyth), Dermot Browne (KPMG Management Consulting), Nic Holt (ICL), Trevor King (Praxis Systems Plc), Tom Lake (GLOSSA), Kathy Spurr (Analysis and Design Consultants), Mario Wolczko (University of Manchester).

Author's preface

Let me start with three facts, some of which you may already have met. Number one: people in business do not want information, they want answers. Number two: research in the USA shows that over 80 per cent of breakdowns in high-tech situations are caused by user error. Number three: the documentation for a Boeing 747 weighs more than the plane itself.

What does this tell you? The answer is simple. Designers, developers, and users of technical products such as computers need documentation. Of course, this can take many forms, and need not necessarily be on paper, but we'll still call it documentation. In this age of 'information overload', people need solutions. Especially in the computer business, people want to use the tools to do their job — how the tools themselves work is not interesting.

This means that there is always a need for people who can write good, clear, structured documentation — the technical writers. They go by many names, such as technical author, software documentation consultant, instructional designer, and so on. But their job is always the same. They must inform, teach, and guide the users of the product concerned, whether it is a highly complex computer system or a household coffee machine.

This book is intended for anyone who is, or going to be, writing software documentation for computer systems. It makes some assumptions about your knowledge of both subjects, but not to too technical a degree. In fact, many of the examples used are not drawn from the computer world at all.

The fact is that many computer companies have their own style and standards for documentation, which are closely guarded secrets. This is fine for them, but I believe that the industry as a whole must work together to produce the right manuals for the customers, as they are currently doing with open systems and joint ventures.

Other companies, in the USA at least, publish their guides for the general public. The only problem with some of these is that they are written for an American audience. I have nothing against Americans, but sometimes their style just does not suit a European readership. However, I must confess my debt to many of these companies for some of the facts and examples I have used in this book.

Many of the books I have read on the subject of documentation make some assumptions about the working practice of the author, which are now out-of-date, in my view. My experience tells me that in most computer companies nowadays the author is not responsible for planning, design, layout, or testing. For this reason, you will find very little about these subjects in the book. I have tried to concentrate on the core tasks: audience analysis, drafting, and editing. However, if you are employed as a one-person organisation, then you will need to find someone to help you with such things as typography. Please do this: your task is to write the documentation, and you should get professional assistance in other areas. I have seen several manuals from small software companies in which the layout and typography were obviously decided upon by someone untrained in these fields, and the result is that much of the really important information is lost in a welter of mixed typefaces and type styles.

Any book on technical writing will never be complete. Writers themselves will recognise this fact: whenever you reread your own work, you find something else to add or change. Nor will any book like this always be up-to-date. For example, while I have included a chapter on online documentation, I have not tried to go into this subject too deeply, as the hardware and software concerned is changing rapidly, and there are already books available on this subject. But I have tried to give a sound basis for writing good, clear documentation, and I hope that the information and advice given here will inform you, entertain you, and guide you.

Another reason why a book such as this will never be up-to-date is the changing nature of user interfaces. From monochrome screens with only capital letters we have arrived at full-colour screens using the Graphical User Interface (GUI). Sound input and output are on their way, and who knows what will be next? The advent of the GUI brought new terms into the user's vocabulary, such as 'radio buttons', 'drop-down lists', and 'check boxes'. The first writers involved in documenting the interface were immediately faced with the problem of how to describe using these features. Do you tell the user to 'click on a button', 'choose a button', or 'use a button'? You may find yourself writing about features that have come to the market after this book was written. Be that as it may, the instructions and advice given here still apply: you may just have to add a few more rules.

I have included some examples of both good and bad writing in the book, as one can always learn from examples. I have also deliberately included some of my personal opinions on writing and styling. You are welcome to disagree with me, of course. The point is that no book is ever written without part of the author's personality showing through. Even when using controlled English (of which more later), there will always be some options which one author will choose and another will not.

Note that, with all due respect to my female readers, I have used the words 'he', 'his', and 'him' in the rest of this book, where I found it impossible to avoid it. I mean no offence, and you should read 'she', 'hers', and 'her' if this is what you prefer (there is more on this subject in the book itself).

I am indebted to HarperCollins Publishers and Penguin Books for providing me with the quotations I have used at the beginning of each chapter.

Martyn Thirlway
September 1993

Acknowledgements

RightWriter is a trademark of Que Software
Grammatik 5 is a trademark of WordPerfect Corporation
Correct Grammar for Windows is a trademark of WordStar International Incorporated
CorrecText is a trademark of Houghton Mifflin Company
PowerEdit is a trademark of a Oracle Corporation
Microsoft, MS-DOS, QuickBASIC, and Windows are trademarks of Microsoft Corporation
WordPerfect is a trademark of Wordperfect Corporation

1   Introduction

'How many good books suffer neglect through the inefficiency of their beginnings?'

Edgar Allan Poe, *Marginalia*

1.1   The aim of writing

What exactly is the purpose of the manual you are about to write? I do not mean what product is it for, but what is the user going to use it for? Well, one can summarise it by describing it as a map. Your reader is going into unknown territory, as far as he or she is concerned, and you are supplying the map.

Of course, you must make sure you draw the map at the right level for your reader to use it successfully. For example, a satellite map of Europe is no use to someone trying to find the way from London to Paris by car. On the other hand, a hiker's map of England and France, showing all the details of each little path, is no use either. What is needed is a reasonably small-scale map, showing the principal towns and cities, and the major roads, together with the distances between each one, and the motorways that join them. If you make this map, then you are supplying just what the intended user needs. This introduces the 'golden rule': if you keep this one in your mind at all times, you cannot go far wrong.

The golden rule is: Always put yourself in the reader's place. The rest of this book shows you different ways of doing this.

1.2   Known problems

Many surveys have been carried out, asking users of software for their opinions of the documentation. Some surveys have concentrated on a product, others on the general quality of the manuals. It seems to me that the results of these surveys can be summarised as follows.

1.2.1   Lack of audience definition

This is caused by one of two things: the writer is not given any information about the user (or fails to look for it), or the writer writes the manual to please the developer or the manager.

1.2.2   Poor structure

This is caused most frequently by one of two things, and sometimes both. The product keeps changing up to the last moment, and the manual structure just 'floats' to keep up. Worse, the writer just jumps in at the deep end and starts writing, without carrying out any definition phase. Information then gets added where it seems to be relevant, and the result is a mess.

1.2.3   Disdain for the reader

This happens when the writer thinks that the user will be impressed by jargon, long complex sentences, and 'talking down'. As one manager is reported to have said, 'If they don't understand this, they're not qualified to read it'. Technical terminology is necessary, but only when a clear English word will not suffice.

1.2.4   Unclear writing

This is often the result of the writer not understanding the subject. The other cause is that the writer uses a style which gets in the way of the reader's understanding of the facts.

1.2.5   Poor use of illustrations

An illustration can get a message across very fast: but only if it is clear, uncluttered, and easy to understand. When illustrations get too complex, the reader can find no way into them, and tends to ignore them, thereby missing what is probably an important piece of information.

1.3   The basic solutions

I assume that you are going to write in English, and that your vocabulary and technical knowledge is at the required level. Having got that out of the way, let's have a quick look at the basic solutions to the problems listed above.

1.3.1   Understand your audience

You must know everything you can about your reader, if you are to succeed in getting your message across. Find out all you can, from whatever sources are available. In this way, you can make the best start, by getting the definition of your book right before you start to write. Chapter 2 tells you more about this activity.

1.3.2   Address the reader directly

As well as using the right vocabulary, how you address the reader is very important. Different readers may need slightly different material, and the way of presenting the information may vary, but only slightly. See Chapter 3 for more information.

The important thing to remember is that you are addressing another human being: a person who wants to understand, as quickly and easily as possible, what you are explaining. Write as you would speak to another person, but avoiding slang, colloquialisms, and jargon. Tell them what they need to know, without trying to impress them. Use simple, everyday words and phrases. Exaggerated formality only gets in the way of understanding. Chapter 5 gives more advice on these subjects.

1.3.3   Keep the information manageable

Break your text up into manageable 'chunks', chapters, sections, and paragraphs. Use short blocks of text that are easy to assimilate, without making the result so 'choppy' that the reader loses the thread or the flow of information. See Chapter 4 for more information on this subject.

1.3.4   Use illustrations wherever possible

Use lists, tables, or figures wherever you can do so, to convey your ideas more clearly or more easily than plain text. Sometimes a table can replace two or more pages of explanatory text, and get the information across faster. Chapter 4 includes information on using lists, and Chapter 6 gives more information on the use of illustrations.

1.3.5   Don't just write, rewrite

When you think you have finished writing, start again. This time, read what you have written, and be your own editor. However good a writer you are, there will always be somewhere to make improvements. Chapter 7 goes into this in more detail.

1.3.6   Give the readers access to what they want

A well-prepared index can make a great difference to a manual. It supplies a fast way for the user to look up information. A glossary of terms can help too, to provide easy access to the terminology being used. Both of these subjects are covered in Chapter 8, together with some advice on preparing appendices.

1.3.7   Make sure that the facts are accurate

Even a well-designed, well-written book is not seen as such unless the facts in it are completely accurate. Manuals need testing as much as the software. Chapter 9 discusses this.

1.3.8 Allow for readability factors

Table 1.1 shows the different readability factors that affect a reader's understanding of printed material. This book does not cover them all, as mentioned earlier, but where you can control the factors, you must of course do so.

Table 1.1 Readability factors

Material	Familiarity of reader with subject matter Relevance to reader's needs/interests (selection) Conceptual difficulty (pitch)
Organisation	Starting tactics: gaining the reader's attention: motivating: orienting Sequence Coherence of argument Unloading rate/density of packing Imposition of pattern, emphasis Balance of exposition/illustration/anecdote Redundancy: unnecessary information versus desirable repetition
Layout	Typeface and size Colour White space Headings Numbering Method of citing references
Relationship between writer and reader	Writer's intention: — teaching — professionally informative — generally informative — light-heartedly informative — humorously entertaining Reader's motivation to learn: — learning — skimming — evaluating Reader's attitudes: — to subject — to journal — to author
Reader's situation	Physical state Physical surroundings Psychological state (mood/memory) Reading ability (speed and accuracy) Social pressures to know/understand/enjoy
Language	Statements/structures (length/complexity) Choice of vocabulary: — verbal/numerical/graphic — familiarity — technical — familiarity — words — familiarity — general words Simplicity/complexity of verb forms and phrasing Punctuation and paragraphing Redundancy: verbosity or desirable repetition Tone created overall (narrative, explanatory, conversational, lecturing, aggressive) Accuracy: of grammar/spelling/punctuation

1.4 Summary

This chapter has suggested various reasons why software documentation is often badly received and some ways to improve the situation. The rest of this book is devoted to giving more detailed advice on these improvements.

2   The first steps

2.1   Introduction

There are six steps in writing a manual, excluding the studying of the product itself. These are:

* Analysing the audience
* Making an outline definition
* Making a detailed definition
* Choosing the style and format you are going to use
* Writing the manual
* Testing the manual.

This chapter deals with the first three steps.

2.2   Analyse the audience

Your book can only be successful if you look carefully at the intended audience before you do anything else. Find out all you can about the intended users of the product you are describing. Then you can start deciding what sort of book they will need. Ask whether similar books already exist: you may be able to make some shortcuts in your design, by using an existing manual as a model.

Let us look at the possible audiences. Figure 2.1 shows a general view of the typical users of a product, to which there may be many exceptions, of course. Not all these manuals will be needed for every subject, and some manual types may be divided into two or more manuals.

2.2.1   Management

The broadest division of the users shown in the diagram is Manager, Technician, and Operator.

Management (also called Administration) activities are carried out by users who establish policies and guidelines, and who make decisions about how the other

User type		Manual type	Reference	Quick reference	Concepts
Management	Business	Quick tour introduction			
Management	Technical	Administrator's guide			
Technician	System	Installer's guide			
Technician	Product	Programmer's guide			
Operator	Skilled	User's guide Operator's guide			
Operator	Unskilled	Getting started			

Figure 2.1 User types and typical manuals

functions are to be performed. We can divide management into business management and technical management.

Business managers are the people who run the company or organisation. They are not necessarily technically minded, but they often have a say in which technology the company uses. This means that they need a summary of what the product can do, so that they can compare it with other similar products. Their introductory manual must be accurate, just like the others, but it can also describe the product in attractive terms. Aimed primarily at the business manager, it may also be read by other users at the start of their activities with the product.

Technical managers are the people who oversee the use of the products, and try to ensure that they are used as efficiently as possible. What they manage depends on the product: one can imagine manuals for Site Administrators, Database Managers, Network Managers, and so on. These manuals must present a lot of information in a clear, straightforward manner. Some of the information may be procedural ('Do this, then that . . .'), some may be guidance ('You will be expected to . . .'), and some may be speculative ('You may find it useful to . . .'). Often you will not have the complete knowledge to write such a book: gathering the necessary information will be a major part of the work.

2.2.2 Technicians

Technicians are those who adapt the purchased product to their own company use, or use it to develop other products. We can divide this category into two sub-categories; system installation and configuration technicians, and product developers.

System installation and configuration technicians deal with complete systems. They may install new releases of software, carry out site preparation, or generate and configure networks, for example. The manuals they need are almost always procedural, giving step-by-step instructions on what to do.

Product developers use one or more products to achieve specific results for the company. Programming is a typical example: the developers use the compilers, interpreters, and other tools to develop a specific tool. These users need both procedural information (*How to use the XYZ compiler*), and reference information (*The M+ Language Reference Manual*).

2.2.3 *Operators and Users*

Operators also fall into two categories: those normally called operators, and those known more generally as users. This does not mean that an operator has more skills than a user, just that they have to perform different tasks. And they both have to learn from the beginning, like everyone else.

Operators carry out tasks that are directly involved with data processing technology. They may be console operators, system operators, or network operators. Like the system developers, they need procedural information, such as when to do what, and how to do it.

Users, on the other hand, should not have to worry about the technology they are using. They need to perform certain business tasks, and their manuals must be very clear and simple, with many examples.

We will be looking at the manual types in greater detail in Chapter 3.

2.3 Make the outline definition

This is one of the most important steps in the whole process. Just as a product cannot be developed without specifications, you cannot write a good manual without first defining what you are going to write. The best novelists are those who make sketches of the plot, the characters, the scenes, and so on, before they start writing.

How you actually produce it is up to you. You may just write it down on paper, or you might want to use a word processor, and a laser printer to make it look better. The point of the outline is that it must enable you, and other people involved, to:

- Check that the book aims at the right audience
- Check that the contents are complete
- Check that the structure is logical
- Get an idea of the book's size and cost.

The form that the outline takes may vary according to the subject matter. At the very least it must satisfy the conditions stated above. This means that it must contain:

- The manual title
- The draft Preface, to show the intended audience
- A draft of the contents list, as detailed as possible
- An estimate of its size.

Depending on whom you work for, it also may be useful to define:

- An estimate of how long it will take to write
- How it will be produced (binding, size, printing methods, and so on)
- An estimate of what it will cost in total.

This enables your management to see what you are proposing to write, what it is going to cost, and when you think it will be ready.

2.3.1 *Choose the manual title*

While we are at this point, let us consider the manual title. It may be that the title of your manual is fixed by your boss, by tradition, or by some other outside influence. If not, you must choose the words carefully to make sure that the title accurately reflects the content of the book. The manual title must indicate its content clearly and simply. Use a short title rather than a long one, but avoid using a title that is so short that it is unclear.

More than once I have seen a programmers' guide called a users' guide (which is not to say that programmers aren't users, of which more later). I have also seen books with titles like *DMOS8* or *PFC Reference*, neither of which says much to the uninitiated.

In spite of manufacturers' different ways of numbering their manuals, most users still refer to them by their titles: the *NITRAM Reference Manual*, or the *XYZ User's Guide*. So your title must be clear. Consider the following three titles, and choose which you think is the best.

Compiler Users' Guide
How to use the C Compiler on the DMOS8 system
DMOS8 C Compiler

I hope you chose the middle one. The first one at least tells you that it is a guide to the usage of the C compiler, but which compiler, and on what system? The last one tells you it is about the C compiler for the DMOS8 system. But it does not say whether it is a technical description, a user guide, or a reference manual. The middle one, however, makes it clear that this book is about how to use the C compiler on the DMOS8 system. It is complete, accurate, and clear.

If you are working on a series of manuals for a particular product, all with similar titles, indicate the intended readership in the title. For example, consider the titles *MR4000 Emulator Installer's Guide* and *MR4000 Emulator User's Guide*.

There may be more manuals about the MR4000 Emulator, but the above titles clearly indicate the intended readership.

Where there is a series of manuals for similar products, the titles should be in a fixed order. For example, with cross-compiler documentation, customers are more likely to have different languages for the same processor rather than one language for different processors. In this case, the first element in the title should be the language.

Note that it is not always necessary to use the word 'manual' or 'guide' in the title. For example, the title *How to install JJ-OS on the MT2901* is clear enough.

2.3.2   *Draft the Preface*

Since we are also already involved with the Preface, let us have a closer look at what it is all about. The purpose of the Preface is to state clearly to the readers:

- Who the book is for
- At what level of experience they are expected to be
- What assumptions the book makes about them
- What other documentation is relevant, if any.

This means that it should be short, and to the point. In your organisation, it is quite possible that there are standard pieces of text that you must use. If this is not the case, just remember the guidelines given above. Remember also that the Preface should not be used to introduce the product, or to explain any technical terms. These subjects should be covered by later parts of the manual, in the appropriate order.

Then, there is the question of describing the structure of the book. There is a continuous debate in technical writing circles about whether this information should be in the Preface or in the first chapter. In my view, this depends on the subject matter.

For example, it is useless to tell the reader that Chapter 4 describes the XYZ primitive, if he will only find out what a primitive is when he reads Chapter 2. In a reference manual, you can describe the structure in the Preface, because you assume that the reader knows the subject matter. In a tutorial or guide, you have to decide. In 'How to use' manuals, you may want to describe the structure after one or two introductory chapters. In a Programmer's Guide, it can be at the beginning. An example of an Outline Definition is given below.

Getting Started with the NITRAM Seat Reservation System
Draft preface
This book is intended for all new users of the NITRAM online seat reservation system.
It assumes that you already know the terms used in airline ticketing, although a short glossary is included at the end, in case you need it.
The book also assumes that you have been instructed in the general use of the terminal that you are going to use. If this is not the case,

then you should first read *How to Use the VEXSTAR Terminal*. Once you have read this book and carried out the exercises described in it, you should have a good idea of the various facilities available to you via NITRAM.

Related documents

NITRAM Seat Reservation System: an overview
How to Use the VEXSTAR Terminal
NITRAM Quick Reference

Contents

ONE Introduction
What NITRAM does
Overview of the features
TWO Starting and stopping NITRAM
How to log on
How to start NITRAM
How to get help
How to stop NITRAM
How to log off
THREE The menu structure
The main menu
The reservations menu
The enquiry menu
FOUR Making reservations
How to book plane tickets
How to book hotels
How to reserve cars
How to print receipts
FIVE How to make enquiries
Flight enquiries
Hotel enquiries
Car hire enquiries
How to print enquiry results
SIX Solving problems
Number of pages: 180
Size: A4, double sided
Binding: 4-ring, standard plastic binder
Production method: Laser printed
Special requirements: Illustrations of menus and data entry screens
Writing: *n* weeks
Illustration: *m* weeks
Cost up to production:
Printing costs:
Production costs:
    per 1000
    per 2000
    per 5000

Notes on the example

The title is, I hope, quite clear. As it says *Getting Started with the NITRAM Seat Reservation System*, the reader can confidently assume that it is the first book to read if he or she needs to use NITRAM.

You will see in the Preface that there is a related manual called *NITRAM Seat Reservation System: an overview*. I have assumed that this is a glossy, promotional piece of literature, and that therefore the average NITRAM user may not have seen it. Had I assumed that they were all introduced to the product via this overview, then the title of the manual in the outline could have been just *Getting Started with NITRAM*.

The opening sentence of the Preface immediately answers the question 'Is this book for me?' or in other words 'I am a new user of this product. Is this the first book I need?' In this way, the readers immediately get an idea of whether or not they should be reading the book in the first place.

The second paragraph says something about the readers' level of knowledge. It implies that it does not explain the airline terminology, but that it uses it. This forces the readers to ask themselves 'Do I know this terminology, and if not, how do I learn it?' In this way, it specifies a level of knowledge that the readers must have, which is not directly computer-related, but is important, nevertheless.

The next paragraph is also about the readers' knowledge, but here it covers the technical knowledge that directly relates to the application concerned.

The last paragraph gives a quick summary of what readers can expect to find in the book, and what they can expect to know when they have finished reading it.

Finally, the list of related documentation gives the readers some context in which they can place this particular manual. A word here about related documents — if you have to give their reference numbers, put the numbers last. As mentioned above, most users refer to their manuals by the titles (or abbreviations of the titles) rather than by the numbers. The numbers are usually only used for ordering purposes.

The contents list at this point does not have any page numbers, for obvious reasons. In addition, I have not numbered anything below the level of the chapters. This is because when I come to write the detailed definition (see below), I may find I want to move sections about, insert a new chapter, or totally resequence the contents.

For example, if the Help feature turns out to need 60 pages of instructions (which would make it a very badly designed Help system!), I could take it out of Chapter 2, and make it a separate Chapter 3, renumbering the remaining ones.

But the contents list so far does give me a good starting point. It does show other people what I am proposing to write, and that is another reason for making the outline.

Of course, this appears to be a very simple system if you read this table of contents. In real life, the table might cover four or five pages.

Once you have drafted your contents list, review it. Check particularly that it covers all the subjects that you have to write about in the book. Make sure that it does not introduce a subject in one chapter that should have been introduced earlier. (On this subject, I have seen many 'Getting started' books that tell you to move the cursor about and press Return in an early chapter. Then later chapters explain what the cursor is, and where the Return key is on the keyboard!)

The last page of the Outline gives an idea of the sort of things to take into account as far as production goes. Of course, you may be forced to use a particular standard, depending on your working environment. But again, estimating this information at the beginning of the writing project at least makes clear to everyone concerned what they are going to get for their money: a very important subject in business.

I have deliberately not put any figures into this part of the Outline, as costs and prices are changing all the time. Depending on your working environment, this information may be supplied by someone else, but that does not mean that you should not include it in the outline definition.

2.3.3   *Make the detailed definition*

Once your outline definition has been accepted, the next step is to make a detailed definition of the book. This is an expansion of the outline definition, and consists of more detailed descriptions of the contents of each chapter, each in perhaps two or three sentences or paragraphs.

This is a very useful step. It gets the information more organised in your head. It can show up problems with the proposed sequence or structure, and gives a better idea of the size of each chapter.

The main effect of making this definition is very often that the Table of Contents changes drastically. This is not a problem: it is a refinement stage before the actual writing. It is also quite possible that more information is available to you at this stage.

Re-examine this definition at least once, and review it with someone else. It is very easy to miss some points, because by now you are getting closer to the subject matter.

Once you have done this, you have a good overview of how the book is going to look when it is finished. The following is a detailed definition of *Getting Started with the NITRAM Seat Reservation System*.

Getting Started with the NITRAM Seat Reservation System
Preface
This book is for all new users of the NITRAM online seat reservation system, who will be responsible for reserving seats, and cancelling and changing reservations.
It assumes that you already know the terms used in airline ticketing, although there is a short glossary at the end, in case you need it.
The book also assumes that you have been instructed in the general use of the terminal that you are going to use. If this is not the case,

then you should first read *How to Use the VEXSTAR Terminal*. This is because this manual uses some terms that are introduced in that book.

Once you have read this book and carried out the exercises described in it, you should have a good idea of the various facilities available to you via NITRAM. If you have any difficulty with the exercises, contact your supervisor.

Related documents

NITRAM Seat Reservation System: an overview

How to Use the VEXSTAR Terminal

NITRAM Seat Reservation: Quick Reference

Contents

ONE Introduction

What NITRAM does

This section introduces the facilities available to the user.

Overview of the features

This section introduces the features of the product itself, such as menus, buttons, the help system, and so on.

TWO Starting and stopping NITRAM

How to log on

How to log on to the central system from the terminal. The use of passwords, and how to change them.

How to start NITRAM, and what the main menu looks like.

How to get help

How to display the context-sensitive help, and how to get back to where you were.

How to stop NITRAM

What to do when you have finished working with NITRAM

How to log off

How to log off from the central system

THREE The menu structure

The menus

How they relate to the main menu

The main menu

How to choose items from this and (stated) other menus

The reservations menu

The principal activities for making reservations, including validation, using a flight as an example

The enquiry menu

The basics of how to carry out enquiries, based on destination, as an example

FOUR Making reservations

Forward reference to enquiries (see below)

How to book plane tickets

The way to do this via start/destination/time/cost/etc.

Special requirements, such as smoking/non-smoking, meals, accompanied minors, non-standard baggage
How to book hotels
Only as an addition to a ticket. Prices/special meals/animals/etc.
How to reserve cars
Only as an addition to a ticket. Prices/agencies/times/rent it here leave it there/etc.
Payment facilities
Cheques/cards/cash, with some warnings
How to print receipts
How to print the receipts for the customer
FIVE How to make enquiries
All these sections can be purely enquiries, can also be used from the reservations menus
Same categories as reservations
Flight enquiries
Hotel enquiries
Car hire enquiries
How to print enquiry results
How to print the results of any enquiry/multiple choices
SIX Solving problems
First a reminder about the Help system
What if no logon possible, NITRAM does not start, and so on?
What if . . . what other problems can occur?
SEVEN Reference section
Quick reference to each activity, showing the principal links between the menus for each activity. Very little text, if any at all.
EIGHT Glossary
Glossary of terms used by NITRAM, not those that are airline-specific (see Preface)
Index
Number of pages: 240
Size: A4, double sided
Binding: 4-ring, standard plastic binder
Production method: Laser printed
Special requirements: Illustrations of menus and data entry screens
Writing: *n* weeks
Illustration: *m* weeks
Cost up to production:
Printing costs:
Production costs:
　per 1000
　per 2000
　per 5000

Notes on the example

Compare this definition to the outline on pages 13 to 15. What has changed? First, I have extended the opening paragraph. It now includes the responsibilities of the audience. This makes it clear that the manual is not for the administrator or manager. I have also extended the third paragraph: it now gives a reason why the reader should have read the book *How to Use the VEXSTAR Terminal*. Because this is a book for a new user, it is possible that the reader will have some difficulties. For this reason, paragraph four now includes some advice on what to do in these cases. One of the titles of the related documents has also changed. In the contents list, I have added a new section at the beginning of Chapter 3. This is because I decided to explain the basics of the menu system itself separately from the main menu, since the principles are the same for all the menus.

At the start of Chapter 4, I have added a forward reference to the enquiry chapter. This is because very often the user will have to make an enquiry before making a booking. As I go further with the book, I may well change the order of Chapters 4 and 5. I have also extended Chapter 4 to include dealing with payments, and receipt printing.

You will see that I have added a reminder to the reader about the Help system at the beginning of Chapter 6. It is quite possible that he or she can solve a problem via the Help system. If not, then they will have to look up the problem in this chapter. I have assumed here that I do not know all the problems that a user may encounter, but at least I have added some obvious details to the definition.

Appendix A and the Glossary are completely new. Appendix A is designed to be a fast reference to the screen menus, with little or no text. This acts as a reminder, without the reader having to reread the chapters concerned. As such, he can use it during further training, if necessary.

I had stated in the Preface that a glossary of terms was included, but had not put it in the table of contents. Now it exists as Chapter 8. I have also added an Index.

Because of the changes, I have also increased the estimated number of pages from 180 to 240. This will have an effect on the cost, so I would have to change that as well.

So I hope it is clear that making this detailed definition is a very useful exercise. It helps you to organise the information before you start. In addition, if it shows up a major change in the times or costs, you have something to show your management. After all, they do not want to be unpleasantly surprised when things take longer than planned, or cost more. So you can use this definition well in advance: they will appreciate it.

Now let us look at the things you must consider when making these definitions, in a little more detail.

2.3.4 Organise the information

When you are preparing your detailed information, you need to remember three important points. You must:

- Consider the product from the user's point of view, rather than that of the developer or analyst
- Make sure that the readers can find the information they need, quickly and easily
- Clearly separate the descriptive, tutorial, and reference information.

1.   *Consider the reader*

Sometimes this is the most difficult part of the entire process of writing a manual. It means that you need to understand the product from the point of the designer and developer, but describe it from the viewpoint of the user — not an easy task.

To take a simple example such as the NITRAM Seat Reservation System, your information may be supplied in the form of descriptions of all the menus, and the possible actions on them. Your job is to describe them in a task-related way, and show the links between them.

Another possibility is that the specifications are grouped into sections called Input, Output, Processing, and Messages. It is clear that this is not the way the user sees the product. For each task the user must carry out, some part of each of these may be relevant.

This is where the audience analysis you carried out earlier proves its usefulness. You know what users want to do with the product, and how they can use it to solve problems and be productive in their work.

You must also consider what their basic tasks are. You must not overload them with too much information in one go. For a tutorial especially, you must concentrate on the simple, basic operation of the software to begin with. You can even leave some of the very complicated tasks to the reference section, as long as this section is clearly laid out in relation to the previous information.

It is quite possible that some of the information in your input specification is irrelevant to the user's tasks — if so, omit it.

2.   *Supply quick access*

Let us start with a basic fact: the average reader of computer manuals does not read them sequentially. They may well read the first one or two chapters, but then they are likely to start jumping from place to place. What they want is to get an idea of what they can do, and start doing it as soon as possible.

Some readers start with the Table of Contents, some with the Index. Others just turn the pages looking for something 'interesting'. There are several ways in which you can make sure that the reader can find what he is looking for, whatever his way of approaching the subject in your book.

- **Table of Contents** To start with, consider the Table of Contents. It must be the right length and balance. A list of chapter titles is not enough. But a list of all the section headings down to the fifth level may be too long, although very often it is a case of the longer, the better. The main aim is to enable the reader to locate minor sections within major ones, down to a reasonable level. For example, in *Getting Started with the NITRAM Seat Reservation*

System it would be ineffective to take the contents list down to the level of 'Entering the airport code' in the chapter on making reservations. This way of accessing information belongs to the Index.

- **Overviews and Summaries** Another way of helping the reader who skins through the manual is to provide overviews and summaries at the start and end of each chapter. These help the user to identify what is in each chapter, and thereby stop and read, or jump to another place in the book.

- **Appendices** If you need to include a lot of tables, which will be rarely referred to, put them into the appendices. But be careful not to put information into appendices that the user will need while reading a particular chapter. This is a guaranteed way to frustrate your reader. If necessary, repeat the information in an appendix for fast access.

- **Glossary** If the product demands a glossary, make a thorough one. Do not include just the new terms, but any that you think the user may want to look up. Another point of frustration is trying to find a definition of something, when the only way is to read parts of the manual, or check all the index entries on that subject. If possible, make a Glossary for the entire product and put it into every book.

- **Index** As mentioned before, some readers start at the back of the book, by looking at the Index. Make sure that you include more than one way of finding the same information, by using synonyms and paraphrasing.

3. *Separate the information*

Depending on the manual you are writing, you may need to include a combination of descriptive, tutorial, and/or reference information. It is very important to separate these, and to make the separation clear.

If you are writing a combined tutorial and reference book, for example, the tutorial must be nothing more than that. The reference part must be separately designed to enable the user to look up information while working, after having completed the tutorial.

It is also the case, as mentioned above, that you can leave some information out of the tutorial, and put it in the reference part. The opposite is not true: the reference part must be complete, as this is where the user will look during day-to-day work.

2.4 Summary

In this chapter we have looked at the first three stages in writing your manual:

- Audience analysis
- Making the outline definition
- Making the detailed definition.

We have considered how to choose a title for the book, and how to construct the Preface. We have also touched on various other subjects, such as the

Appendices, Glossary, and Index, all of which are covered further in Chapter 8.

Here is a summary of the questions you must ask yourself when carrying out these first steps.

- Who is going to use this book?
- What are they going to use it for?
- Does the reader already know anything about the subject?
- What is the main purpose of the book?
- Does it have any other purpose?
- What information should I include?
- What information should I leave out?
- How long is it going to take to write?
- Will it need special illustrations?
- How much is it going to cost to produce?

If you have the answers to all these questions, you are well on the way. The next stage is to consider what style of writing and presentation you are going to use, depending on the type of book you are writing. The next chapter tells you how to do this.

3   The types of books

'The better the book the more room for the reader'
Holbrook Jackson, Maxims of Books and Reading

3.1   Introduction

Chapter 1 mentioned the six steps in the writing process:

- Analysing the audience
- Making an outline definition
- Making a detailed definition
- Choosing the style and format you are going to use
- Writing the manual
- Testing the manual.

This chapter deals with the fourth step, choosing the style and format to suit your audience and the type of book you are going to write.

There are four kinds of manual available to software users:

- Introductory manuals
- Training manuals
- User manuals
- Reference manuals

These categories cover more than just four possible books, however. For example, a Programmer's Guide and a 'How to use...' manual are both User manuals. A complete Reference manual and a Quick Reference booklet are both types of Reference manuals.

You can, of course, combine these types in one book, as mentioned earlier. A training manual may have a reference part as well, for example. There are other possibilities which may or may not be available to you, such as wall charts or pull-out posters.

This chapter deals with the audience, the purpose, and the general content of each of the four types mentioned above. This information is to help you check that what you are about to write is going to be what the user wants. After that you can start the writing itself.

The content and style of the book depends on the type of user you are writing for. Using your detailed definition and the manual descriptions given in this chapter, you can plan the content and style for your particular book. Later chapters describe the various elements making up each book type (except for the Preface, covered in Chapter 2).

3.2   Introductory manuals

Introductory manuals have two possible audiences. The first is a potential customer who is considering whether to buy the product. The second is one who has the product, but does not know anything about it yet (a word processor operator is a good example).

3.2.1   Purpose

The purpose of such a manual is to give a general overview of the product, and to emphasise the benefits to be gained from using it. It should therefore describe the product features that are of most interest to the reader. It may be the next book they read after a sales brochure.

3.2.2   Content

The book must provide a general overview of the product, and describe each feature at a more detailed level. You should include a summary of the main points at the end.

3.2.3   Style

The style of an Introductory manual must be light. This does not mean that the treatment should not be serious, but rather that the reader must want to continue reading.

3.3   Training manuals

By a Training manual, I mean a book for new users, to help them learn what to do. New users, in this context, means those who are new to the product or service you are describing. Of course, they also may be new to computers, and you may need to take this into account as well. Because of their lack of experience, they may well have anxieties or worries about using the product. They may be afraid of doing something wrong, or worry that they will never master the product.

   Some of them may have been told by their boss to use it, with no other help or encouragement. Alternatively, they may be keen to use the product, and get acquainted with it as quickly as possible. This is often the case with non-computer-oriented managers, who just want to use the tools they have bought. So, as you can see, you can define this audience up to a certain point, but often you cannot define the new user in any exact detail. In any case, your job is to allay any fears they may have, and lead them gently into the subject matter. Let's summarise all this in a more formal way.

3.3.1 Purpose

The purpose of a Training manual is to introduce the user to the system or product. The book must take the place of a teacher, but must allow the reader to learn at their own pace. It must confirm that they are doing it right, and help them when they go wrong. It must also give them confidence, so that they can go on to become experienced. If it fails in this aspect, it will leave them in a more worried state than when they began. Their boss will no doubt still expect them to be able to do the job, however.

It should enable them to carry out the basic tasks, after one pass through the book. If they have to refer to it several times to carry out the basics, then the book has missed its mark.

3.3.2 Content

The content must be a series of lessons, each one building on the one before it. It is important to give an overview of each lesson, to tell the reader what they are going to learn next. In addition, make sure you make it clear how to break off in the middle, and carry on later.

Each lesson should contain a limited amount of information. Usually, such a manual should never attempt to explain everything about the product, as this will be too overwhelming for the reader. In addition, if the user 'discovers' another way of doing something, they will feel confident — they won't complain that you did not mention it.

3.3.3 Style

Use a simple and repetitive style, and a reassuring (but not compromising) tone. You should write detailed step-by-step instructions, and try to anticipate possible mistakes that the user might make.

Teach the ideas from specific cases. You could perhaps draw a scenario, in which the reader plays a part. If you do this, make the examples as real as possible.

Keep the audience firmly in mind. An experienced word processor user who is learning about a new word processor needs help on the operational aspects. A reader who has not used a word processor previously will need guidance and help in the concepts and the operation. A business manager learning about a spreadsheet calculator will want to be working as soon as possible, preferably within about 20 minutes from starting your book.

Above all, don't leave any 'what if?' questions in the reader's mind.

3.4   User manuals

By User manual, I mean a manual for the intermediate level users. These people are more aware than the users of the Training manuals. They may well have experience with computers, and even with products similar to the one you are dealing with.

If they have learned via the Training manual, they are now looking for more information. In any case, you can rest assured that they do not need their 'hands held' in the same way as the users of the Training manual.

3.4.1 Purpose

The purpose of the User manual is to introduce all the capabilities of the system. It should not only do this, but the emphasis should also be on showing the reader what the product can do for him. This does not mean that it is in any way a sales brochure: it must be the opposite. It must not tell the reader what the product can do, but how he can use the product to do what he wants.

This does not mean that you should just describe all the various possibilities, but you must also aim at showing how to achieve results with the product (see also Section 3.7, 'Task-based structure'). In cases where there is more than one way to get the desired result, mention them all.

3.4.2 Content

The content of the User manual must focus on results and how to get them. You must organise the topics in a logical way. The manual must be comprehensive, although you can leave out more complex or more technical features that you consider too advanced for intermediate users.

3.4.3 Style

The style should be somewhere between a Training manual and the next category, Reference manuals. To this end, it is quite acceptable to have quite a lot of descriptive headings. This may appear at first glance to break up the flow of the text. However, the convenience of quickly locating specific subjects justifies the sort of 'choppiness' generated by the headings.

Present the information in a general way, and allow the reader to apply their knowledge to more detailed situations.

If there is no associated Reference manual, then you must include all limits, values, parameters, messages, and so on. You can detail them in the narrative part, or put them into a reference section at the end of the book.

3.5   Reference manuals

The users of the Reference manuals have more knowledge of the product than the users in the other two categories. According to my definition, they are computer literate, and are already familiar with the system or product.

However, they are not necessarily familiar with all the possibilities of the product. They may have a working knowledge or more than a working knowledge, but want (or need) to know more. Or they may want to look up a particular item that they cannot quite remember during their day-to-day work.

3.5.1 *Purpose*

It follows, then, that the purpose of a Reference manual is to provide the facts, all the facts, and in an easy-to-find, unambiguous way.

3.5.2 *Content*

So it is the Reference manual that is 'the Bible' about the product. It must be structured in such a way that facts can be found quickly and easily, and it must be complete. Organise the subject matter in a logical way, by function, or alphabetically, depending on how you expect your reader to search for the information.

3.5.3 *Style*

Present the facts, in a straightforward manner, so that your readers can look up what they want to know and apply it to their current work. Use a descriptive, matter-of-fact tone. Focus on the capabilities, and leave out the 'nice to know' type of information, as your reader just wants the facts.

The manual must be command- or function-oriented, and should be designed for quick access. Use selective repetition to prevent the reader looking something up in the index, and being directed from the referenced page to another place in the book.

The book must have a complete, comprehensive index, unless you have organised it in alphabetic order. Even then you may need to make an index to include synonyms (see Chapter 8 for more information on Indexes).

3.6 Examples

The following are four examples of descriptions and instructions of the same (imaginary) product, taken from the Introductory manual, the Training manual, the User manual, and the Reference manual.

3.6.1 *The Introductory manual*

> With NiteMail, everyone who has access to a VEXSTAR terminal can make multiple copies of memoranda, minutes, reports, or any kind of document, and mail them to other users of the system — instantly. Just like an ordinary postal system, each NiteMail user has an address in the system, which is unique. So to direct a document to another user, you just choose their address. You can also send mail to several users at once, or to all the users in a particular part of the organisation. You can request confirmation of delivery, and ask the recipients to reply to your mail by a certain date, and the NiteMail service will remind them until they do.

3.6.2 *The Training manual*

Sending mail
Use the Send option to send a NiteMail message to one or more
users. You can request confirmation of delivery, and ask the
addressee(s) to reply by a certain date.

1. Select the document to be sent.
2. Choose Send from the Desktop menu. NiteMail displays the
    address list.
3. Select the address from the list, and click on the Add button.
    You can also select more than one address by clicking on each
    one in turn to select or deselect it.
4. Click on the Request Confirmation box if you want to be
    informed when the mail has been delivered.
5. Click on the Request Reply box if you want to ask for a reply.
    NiteMail opens a separate window for you to enter the date
    by which you want the reply.
6. Click on Send to send the mail.

3.6.3 *The User manual*

Distributing documents
Using the NiteMail facility, you can send documents and messages
to other users and organisational blocks. You can also send mail
to users via fax, if the necessary facilities are available on your
system.

Internal mail
When you send mail to another user, you can choose one of the
following mail modes.

- *Forward* If you use Forward mode, the document is removed
  from your desk and placed in the Mail Inbox of the addressee.
- *Copy* If you use Copy mode, the document is copied once for
  every user you specify, and one of these copies is sent to each
  user.

External mail
When you sent mail via fax, it is always sent in Forward mode.

Using Send
Use this option to send a document. You can send the mail to one
or more addressees, including users and organisational blocks. You
can select the Request Reply and Request Confirmation options,
and you must also select one of the mail modes described above.

1. Select the document to be sent.

> 2. Choose Send from the Desktop menu. NiteMail displays the address list.
> 3. Select the addresses from the list, and add them to the distribution list.
> 4. Set the Request Confirmation option on if you want to be informed when the mail has been delivered.
> 5. Set the Request Reply option on if you want to ask for a reply, and enter the date by which you want the reply.
> 6. Select the mode required (Forward or Copy).
> 7. Use Send.

3.6.4 The Reference manual

> **Sending Mail**
> Desktop Menu → Send
> Select Addresses + Add
> [Check Request Confirmation]
> [Check request Reply (Enter date)]
> [Select Mode Forward/Copy]
> Send

3.7 Task-based structure

All the above manuals have one thing in common: they are to help people carry out certain tasks. This means that you, as the writer, must make your manual fit the tasks of the user, not the structure of the product — and usually not the structure of the specification.

This means thinking about the way in which the user will work with the product. The specification may be organised in a certain way, but its intended readership is a very different one from the manual you are writing. I have seen an example of this for an Office Automation system. There was a complete series of books on how to use the various components. What the user needed was a book covering the linking of the components as a whole to the user's job, and this did not exist.

3.8 Summary

This chapter has covered the different types of manuals, together with their audiences, purposes, and an idea of their styles. Together with the detailed definition, you now have enough material to start the actual writing process. The following chapters describe this.

4 Writing the first draft

'Boozing does not necessarily have to go hand in hand with being a writer . . .
I therefore solemnly declare to all young men trying to be writers that they do
not actually have to become drunkards first'

James Jones, in an interview in *Writers at Work*

4.1 Introduction

You will remember the six steps in the writing process, mentioned in Chapter 1:

- Analysing the audience
- Making an outline definition
- Making a detailed definition
- Choosing the style and format you are going to use
- Writing the manual
- Testing the manual.

This chapter describes the fifth of these steps, the basics of the writing process;
you will see more details of this process in later chapters. It also gives some advice
on chapters and appendices, headings, and cross-references. But to start with,
here are three more rules to remember while you are writing.

- **Keep in touch with your editor** Some companies have editors, others don't.
  If you have an editor, make friends with him or her. Good editors are few
  and far between, so make all the use of them you can. If possible, give your
  editor the outline of your book at the very start of the process. Then give him
  the detailed definition. If you are having a problem in expressing some thought,
  go and ask for advice. Perhaps he will come up with a way of describing
  something that you had not considered — it is very easy to be in the state of
  'can't see the wood for the trees' while you are writing, and the last thing
  you want is for your reader to end up in the same state.

  (A word here about the editor/writer relationship. It is important that you,
  as a writer, do not consider your first draft of a book to be written on tablets
  of stone. Editing is carried out for a variety of reasons (see Chapter 7, Rewrite
  and edit). While some of the reasons are clarity, consistency of terminology,
  and good English, really good editors can put themselves in the place of your

reader. In doing this, they may ask questions that you had not thought of, they can find problems with your explanations, and so on.)

- **Review continuously**   Every time you write a chapter, read it! I cannot count the number of manuals I have come across that have been written, but never read, by the author. Take pride in what you write. If you read something you have written, you will always find that you can improve it. It is happening to me while I write this, but of course at some stage one has to stop and deliver the goods. At the same time, once you have finished, you can apply the rules given in Chapter 7 to further improve the result.
- **Learn from your mistakes**   When you read something you have just written, you will very often make corrections to it immediately. When you do, take note of what you are doing. Then, when you come to write the next part, you can avoid those problems as you go along. If necessary, make notes for yourself on a piece of paper, and keep them handy.

4.2   Doing the actual writing

In spite of all of the above, you have got to get on with the writing itself, of course. So, while applying the above rules, don't worry about anything else, such as spelling. Write the way you would if you were verbally explaining something to a user, and you cannot go far wrong.

Based on your detailed definition, you already have the structure defined, and all you have to do is fill in the gaps with the actual information. Study the product or the specification, in more detail, and make sure that you understand what you are going to write in each chapter or section. Then go for it. Just write, write, write, until you get to the end.

Of course, you may well come across something that is not completely clear. Don't stop to worry about it. Put in a piece of text that says 'more information needed' or something similar, and keep going. If you break off what you are doing to go and seek out that little bit of information, it will break your train of thought, and with it the continuity of your writing.

For example, I was recently documenting a software package, in which the administrator has to enter a country code. I wrote the instructions, but had no idea what codes were possible. Rather than stop and find out, I wrote the sentence 'Appendix A lists the possible country codes', and carried on. When it later turned out that there were only four codes, I was able to replace the sentence with a list of the codes themselves. If you work in this way you should make a separate note of the references, so that you remember to check them later.

4.3   Chapters

Chapters are the main divisions of information in a book. The whole point of dividing a book into chapters is to make it easy for your readers to find what they are looking for.

Chapters are collections of related material, and should be similar in length and importance. A one-page chapter is too abrupt and superficial: a fifty-page chapter may be too long. Try to present similar information at the same level, and keep related topics together, even when this results in short or long chapters. If you are working on a series of books, apply the same structure to all of them, whenever possible.

There is no point in using a chapter structure when the majority of a book is one chapter. In this case it is possible to make the book without chapters.

All this means that you may find that the detailed definition of the book cannot be reflected in the actual material, once you have started writing. But don't worry about that; the most important thing is that the end result is usable by the reader.

4.4   Sections and subsections

A section is a subdivision of a chapter that you use to break up the chapter into digestible pieces. A section should cover one activity, and only one. This enables the reader to 'jump' more easily to a particular point in the chapter, especially if your sections have clear, meaningful titles.

If necessary, you can also use subsections. These are only needed if the related section is very long, on account of the subject it covers. Again, give your subsections meaningful titles.

4.5   Paragraphs

A paragraph is a group of sentences that supports and develops a single idea. You must use paragraphs to provide a logical break in the material, and to create physical breaks on the page, which help the reader to absorb the information.

In general, you should begin a new paragraph whenever you describe or introduce a new idea, subject, time, or place. A page divided into a number of paragraphs is easier to read and understand than one consisting of one large piece of undivided text. At the same time, do not use lots of small paragraphs.

Never split a paragraph over a page break. If necessary, split the paragraph in two: otherwise, put the whole paragraph on the next page. Always leave one blank line between paragraphs.

4.6   Appendices

An appendix provides information which is additional or supplementary to the main body of the book. It should not contain information which is essential to the reader's understanding of the rest of the book. At the same time, if you are writing appendices, you should treat them in the same way as chapters, using the same standards and structure. For more information on writing appendices, see Chapter 8.

4.7 Headings

When you write your book, you structure it in the way you think best for the reader. Your choice of headings is equally important, because the reader uses them to get an idea of what is coming next. Headings 'set the scene'.

The number of heading levels you are allowed to use depends on the department or company you work for. Most allow three levels (the chapter, the main section, and the subsection), but some allow more. My personal preference is not to go to any further depth in the structure. I feel that if I need a subsubsection, then I have not structured the information correctly. Perhaps I need to split the chapter into two or three smaller ones, thereby raising all the information by one heading level.

A heading should be as self-contained as possible. This means that on meeting a subsection heading, your reader must not have to reread the section heading to understand the subsection heading.

The heading must be relevant to the content of the section or subsection. If the heading does not clearly define what is in the section, it is inadequate. At the same time, try to make your headings as brief as possible. Never write a heading that is longer than one line. Always put some text between a section heading and the first subsection heading.

In addition, make sure that you are consistent in the way you use headings. Once you have been given a rule, or defined one for yourself, stick to it. My own rules are these. A chapter heading can be followed by either text or a section heading. A section heading or subsection heading must be followed by text. This means that I never follow a section heading immediately with a subsection heading (except in this book).

Be consistent in the wording of headings, as well. For example, if you use the heading 'Using the System', then use 'Entering Data', not 'Using the System' and 'How To Enter Data'. Be consistent in the use of capitals in headings as well. Do not use capitals for one heading and a mixture of lower case and capitals for another heading at the same level.

Use a verb (preferably the gerund) for a heading to a section that describes a procedure: for example, 'Sending Mail'.

Use a noun, preceded by an appropriate article, for a heading to a section that describes an item (such as a piece of software). For example, 'The Desktop Menu'.

You may or may not be asked to include numbers in your headings. These are normally made up of the chapter number, followed by the section number, in the form '2.1', or '2.1.3' for a subsection. Personally, I hate seeing these numbers in headings. I expect to be able to find what I want in the manual via the Table of Contents or the Index, or by reading consecutive sections. This means that the numbers in the headings mean nothing to me, and can detract from the speed of my reading and understanding of the headings themselves. (You will note that this book uses numbered headings: this is because I wrote it to a predefined style, which is, after all, part of my job!)

Depending on your standards, you may have to follow some rules about case.

If you write your headings in lower case, be careful with trademarks and copyrighted names. For example, 'WordPerfect' must be written in lower case with a capital W and a capital P.

4.8   Cautions and warnings

Use the word 'CAUTION' to alert the reader to any procedure or operation that could cause equipment damage or loss of data. Use the word 'WARNING' where the procedure could cause physical injury (see Box 4.1).

Make sure that you put the caution or warning **before** the dangerous step. I have seen more than one manual which gives detailed step-by-step instructions over a page or more, and then the warning comes last.

<table>
<tr><td>CAUTION If you have a fixed disk, use SHUTDOWN before moving your PC.
WARNING Before opening the cabinet, make sure the PC is switched off and the mains cable is unplugged.</td><td>Box 4.1</td></tr>
</table>

4.9   Examples

Highlight examples clearly. Use the word 'Example' before the example text, and make it clear where the example starts and ends. When there is more than one example, number each example separately as 'Example 1', 'Example 2', and so on. This enables the reader to identify the beginning of each example. Always start each new set of examples with the number '1'. Where the example is the continuation of a sentence in the main text, use the phrase 'for example' or something similar.

When you are writing examples, remember that the reader of your book may be of any nationality. This means that you must make the examples as international as possible. For example, use Amsterdam, London, and Paris, not London, Birmingham, and Glasgow.

You may also need to include sample names, addresses, and so on as part of an imaginary installation. Again, you should make these as international as possible. In the United States and Canada especially, the mix of names that come from the old immigrant families lead to some surprising (to the British) combinations. The Appendix at the end of this book gives some sample names and addresses that you can use as a 'pick and mix' to make your own examples.

4.10   Notes

You can use a note to inform the reader of important or additional information to the subject being described. When there is more than one note, number each note separately, in the same way as examples (see Box 4.2).

Note 1. If you send mail to a fax number, it is always sent in copy mode.
Note 2. You may only use fax numbers that have been pre-installed. You may not enter one that does not appear in the list.

4.11 Cross-references

4.11.1 General rules

Most cross-references refer the reader to another manual, chapter, or section for additional or related information. Whenever you refer to anything, make your meaning clear by including the words 'manual', 'guide', 'chapter' or 'section'.

You can refer the reader to another page, but I would strongly recommend that you do not do this in books of more than 10 or 12 pages. This is because when a book is updated, the page numbers may change, and if the book is translated, the page breaks can change (this is a common occurrence when translating from English to other European languages). Your page references will then be wrong.

Cross-references can also refer to a figure or table, but be careful with these. If the figure or table is relevant to the understanding of the text you are writing, it is often better to repeat the figure or table, rather than refer to it. In this way, your reader does not have to turn to another page to see the figure, and then back again.

You may have a style that you must apply to cross-references. Some companies use quotation marks, others use italics, others use small capitals. Personally, I prefer to use italics for the actual reference, as shown in Box 4.3.

The format of the reference is largely up to you. Unless you already have a standard, choose from the following:

There is more information about this in section . . .
See . . . for more information.
Chapter *N* gives you more information.
For more information, see . . .
Chapter *N* describes . . . in more detail.
You can find more information in . . .

You can find more information in Chapter 7, *Installing a trackball.*
Chapter 3 describes the login procedure in more detail.
See Table 6, *Country Codes,* for the possible values for this parameter.

Whichever you choose, use the same format consistently.

4.11.2   *Referring to other manuals*

To refer the reader to another manual, give the full title of the manual, using the same capitalisation as is used in the manual itself. If the manual referred to belongs to another product line or manufacturer, include the product line or manufacturer as well (see Box 4.4).

There is more information on this subject in the *Getting Started with WhizWorks* manual. See Microsoft's *QuickBASIC* manual for more information.

Box 4.4

You can also use a 'See under' reference to a section in another manual. Any manual you refer to in the manual you are writing must be listed in the Related manuals or Related publications section in the Preface. See Chapter 2, 'The first steps', for more information about writing the Preface.

You may also want to refer to a specific chapter in another manual. In this case, follow the rule for manuals, but do not include the chapter number. You never know when the other manual is going to change, and the number may then be incorrect (see Box 4.5).

See the chapter 'Starting the System' in the *WhizWorks System Administrator's Guide*.

Box 4.5

4.11.3   *Referring to other chapters*

To refer to another chapter in the same manual, use the chapter number and the title, rather than just the number. The number tells your reader whether the chapter is before or after the one they are currently reading. If your manual has running heads, readers can scan these for the chapter title, rather than going back to the Table of Contents to find where the chapter starts.

To refer the reader to an appendix in the same manual, use the word 'Appendix' with a leading capital, followed by the upper-case letter (or the number) of the appendix. You can include the appendix title in the reference. In this case, use the same style as you do for referring to chapters. It is usually best not to refer the reader to sections in an appendix. For more information on appendices, see Chapter 8, 'Writing the appendices, glossary, and index'.

You can also refer to the 'previous' and 'next' chapters, but you should still include the title in the reference.

4.11.4   *Referring to other sections*

As with chapters, give the section number (if relevant), and the full text of the section or subsection title. To refer to a section that has already occurred in the same chapter, use the words 'earlier in this chapter'.

To refer to a section that occurs later in same chapter, use the words 'later in this chapter'. You can also refer to the 'previous' or 'next' section. In Box 4.6 I have used single quotes to highlight the section titles, but if you have a different standard, of course you must follow that.

Box 4.6

> See 'Starting WhizWorks' later in this chapter for more information. For more information, see 'Starting WhizWorks' later in this chapter.

To refer to a section in a different chapter, add the words 'in Chapter *N*', where *N* is the chapter number, and give the chapter title (see Box 4.7).

Box 4.7

> See 'Starting WhizWorks' in Chapter 2, *Working with WhizWorks*, for more information.

4.12   Text formats

Although I have stated that you should just get on with the writing, it is worth remembering that there are various ways you can get your message across in text, apart from sentences and paragraphs. These include:

- Hyphen or bulleted lists
- Numbered lists
- Dialogues
- Keyword lists.

First let us look at these different ways of presenting information, and then consider which ones are best suited for the three manual types previously defined.

4.12.1   Hyphen or bulleted lists

These can be used as a variation on prose. But you should not make lists for the sake of it: very often, clear well-written prose can in fact do the job better. Use a list when you need to break up a sentence that would otherwise be long and difficult to follow. Lists are especially useful when you are describing a choice of actions or results (see Box 4.8).

Box 4.8

> You can use the user administration tool to add new users, change existing users, reset passwords, deactivate and reactivate users, and assign user profiles.
> You can use the user administration tool to:
>
> - Add new users
> - Change existing users
> - Reset passwords

> - Deactivate users
> - Reactivate users
> - Assign user profiles.

Note that the order of the list items may be alphabetic or in order of importance. It may also be in a logical order, such as 'adding', 'changing', and 'deleting', which by a happy coincidence is also alphabetic.

You can also use lists to describe a checklist, as in Box 4.9.

> Before you start, make sure that you have the following items available.
>
> - The new thermostat
> - The small rubber hose
> - A small screwdriver.

Box 4.9

4.12.2 Numbered lists

Use numbered lists when describing a series of steps the user must take, where the order of the steps is important. Box 4.10 shows a list where the steps must be carried out in the order shown.

> To install the new version, do the following.
>
> 1. Put the diskette in drive A.
> 2. Open the File Manager menu.
> 3. Choose the Run option.
> 4. Type **a:install** in the Command Line field.
> 5. Click on OK.

Box 4.10

You should also use numbered lists when you want to refer from one step to another, or you want to be able to make the reader miss a step, as shown in Box 4.11.

> 1. Choose Users from the Administration menu.
> 2. Choose Add from the User menu.
> 3. Enter the user name
> 4. If you are adding an external user, go to step 6.
> 5. Enter the workstation number. Go to step 7.
> 6. Enter the routing number.
> 7. Click on OK to save the details.

Box 4.11

Be very careful when writing jumps from one step to another, to make sure that nothing is missed. Test all the jumps yourself. It is very easy, when the text for each step is more than one paragraph, to put the jump entry points in the wrong place.

4.12.3 Dialogues

You can use dialogues to demonstrate the interaction between the user and the computer. Dialogues are a useful way of showing what the user must do, and how the system responds. This is best shown by Box 4.12.

Box 4.12

Action	Response
Enter: DISKCLN	Disk clean: disk number?
Enter: 2	Confirm clean disk 2?
Enter: Y	Cleaning . . .
	Clean another disk Y/N?
Enter: N	Utility ended

This example is obviously contrived for illustration purposes, but in some circumstances this is a very useful way of presenting instructions clearly and concisely.

You may need another way of presenting dialogues, when you need to describe what is happening as well as what the reader must do. You can use the format shown in Box 4.13, which combines a numbered list with a dialogue format.

Box 4.13

6. You must tell the system which database to use.
   System: DATABASE NAME?
   Enter: demo
7. You must then give the password.
   System: PASSWORD?
   Enter: demo

4.12.4 Keyword lists

You can use keyword lists when telling your reader what they must enter into a form or dialogue box on the screen. Often, some fields are already filled in, and others must be completed by the reader. In some cases, the reader can change a field that is already filled in with a default value (see Box 4.14).

Box 4.14

In this dialogue box, you must fill in the details of how you want the file to be printed.
Document   Enter the name of the document, if it is not
             already filled in.

Copies	This is preset to 1. If you want more than one copy, enter a number in the range 2−99.
Page range	This is preset to 'All'. If you want to print a single page, enter the page number here.
Destination	This is preset to the name of your printer. If you want to send the output to a different printer, or to a file, enter the new name here.

4.12.5 *Using the right formats in the manuals*

Not all the formats we have just seen are necessarily the right one for each type of manual. We identified three types of manual:

- Training
- User
- Reference

Table 4.1 shows which types of formats are best suited to each of the manual types.

4.12.6 *Documenting procedures*

We have just seen some different ways of documenting steps that the user must take. Whichever one you choose, remember that there are some rules to go with all of them, as follows.

Choose the layout that makes the instructions most easily understood and followed. Never assume anything on your reader's part. You are instructing your readers on what to do, and you cannot assume that they know anything, except what you have previously described in the book. Use familiar analogies to help explain complicated steps. Describe all the steps in a logical way. In other words, where the sequence of the steps is not important, choose an order that makes the most obvious sense. Start each instruction with a command verb, such as 'Type', 'Enter', and so on.

If the procedure is very complex, and has many possible paths through it, start with a summary of what the reader is going to have to do, and what choices he or she is going to have to make (see Box 4.15).

Table 4.1 Text formats and manual types

Training manual	User manual	Reference manual
Prose	Prose	Prose
	Lists	Lists
Numbered lists	Numbered lists	
Dialogues	Dialogues	
Keyword lists	Keyword lists	Keyword lists

Choose New Booking from the main menu. The transaction number is allocated automatically, and the Flight Reservation screen is displayed. If you want to skip this, press 'H' for Hotel, or 'A' for Auto (see steps 9–15 and 16–21 below for further details of how to handle these reservations).

Flight reservation
1. Choose the departure point from the DEP scrolling list, by double-clicking on it.
2. Choose the destination from the ARR scrolling list, by double-clicking on it.
3. Choose the day from the DAY list, by double-clicking on it. A secondary window opens, listing all the flights between the departure and destination points for that day of the week. Note that flights shown in grey are already fully booked, which means that you cannot select them.
4. Double-click on the flight required.
5. Enter the number of passengers in the NOP field.
6. Enter the name of the (first) passenger in the NAME file. If there is more than one passenger, press TAB to open a further empty line for this field.
7. Ask the customer to confirm that what they see on their screen is what they require. If so, click on CONFIRM. The Hotel Reservation screen is displayed. Go to step 9, below.
    If not, move the cursor to the field to be changed, and press the right mouse button. Then follow the instructions given above for the field.
    If you want to restart the entire booking, click on RESTART.
    If you want to cancel the transaction, click on CANCEL.

4.12.7 Documenting messages

Here is a subject that I could write more than a dozen pages on, as it is one of my pet hates. I have seen so many manuals that either do not explain any messages that the user may see, or provide a list of them without any explanations at all. The worst case, from a large European computer manufacturer, was a manual of ten chapters, in which Chapter 7 was called 'Messages'. This chapter consisted of a one-page list of messages, not in any particular order, and with no explanatory text whatsoever.

Messages are part of the user interface. This means that you should try to influence the developer, if possible, to choose sensible message texts. Not only does this make the interface better, but it also cuts down on the amount of explanation you have to give in your book.

For example, if a message says 'Illegal function key', try to get it changed to 'You may not use that function key now'. Change 'No file found' to 'File [filename] not found in specified directory', to give another example. However, do not give the software its own personality, using messages such as 'I cannot find your file'.

Make sure that you obtain a complete list of possible messages, and, if you do not understand any yourself, ask the developer — do not guess the meaning. Organise them into a logical order. If they all start with a number, list them in numerical sequence, otherwise list them in alphabetic sequence.

In some cases it may be worth grouping them into categories such as 'Log in messages', 'Mail messages', and so on. This depends largely on the nature of the product, and the total number of messages.

Add a clear explanation to each message, and give some advice on what the user must do to solve the problem, even if the advice is 'No action is required' (see Box 4.16).

CP0073	**The new password you have entered is not allowed.**	Box 4.16
Reason	The new password you have specified conflicts with the rules for passwords on your system. Passwords must be at least four characters long, and must begin with a letter (A–Z).	
Action	Enter a valid password. If you need more information, contact your NITRAM Administrator.	
ETR1154	**You cannot change the ownership of a transaction that is not yours**	
Reason	You cannot change the ownership of a transaction that you did not create yourself.	
Action	If you really need to do this, you must either contact the current owner of the transaction, or ask your NITRAM Adminstrator for help.	
ETR2087	**You cannot do this now, because someone else is working on the transaction**	
Reason	Another operator is currently working on this transaction.	
Action	Try again later, or contact the operator involved. If you need more help, contact your NITRAM Administrator.	
LG0001	**You are already logged in**	
Reason	You have already logged in to NITRAM on this or another workstation.	
Action	If you have already logged in on this workstation, press ESC to clear this message, and then switch to NITRAM.	
	If you are logged in at another workstation, you must first log out on that workstation, and then press	

	ENTER to clear this message and log in at this workstation.
	If you are unsure of what to do, or you do not think you have already logged in, contact the NITRAM Administrator.
LG0002	**Invalid log in, please try again**
Reason	You have entered an incorrect user name or password. The message does not tell you which is incorrect, for security reasons.
Action	Log in again, making sure that you enter the name and password assigned to you by the NITRAM Administrator, or contact him if you are not sure what to do.

4.13 Summary

This chapter has concentrated on ways of presenting information to match the target audience. It has also dealt with the various text elements that you can use to structure your book in a clear way. In addition, it has covered two of the subjects that users need most: procedural instructions, and explanations of messages. At this stage, we have established the audience of the book, the contents, and the different text elements that we can use when writing. The next chapter deals with the style of presenting the information within the defined structure.

5 Style

'When we see a natural style, we are quite surprised and delighted, for we expect to find an author and we find a man'

Blaise Pascal, *Pensées*

5.1 Introduction

This chapter covers the more detailed parts of the writing, from problems in sentence construction to representing numbers in text. The chapter is divided into sections on:

- Using the right tense
- Clarity
- Controlled English
- Sentence length
- Pompous style
- Technical terms and jargon
- Variety and inconsistency
- Numbers in text
- Using highlighting (bold, italic, and so on)
- Capitalisation
- Colloquialisms and slang
- Humour
- Using 'he' or 'she'
- Using 'must', 'should', 'can', and 'may'
- Acronyms and abbreviations
- Punctuation.

You will find that there many examples of bad writing in this chapter (in the boxes, of course). Study them carefully. If you recognise any of them as part of your style, change your style according to the rules given in each section.

5.2 Using the right tense

5.2.1 Introduction

You can enhance your writing style by the consistent use of the proper verb tense.

Most books you write should be written in the present tense. You can sometimes use the past tense when communicating background information. You should only use the future tense when describing the expected results of particular actions.

In grammar, the term 'voice' refers to the way the subject is related to the action expressed by the verb. If the subject is the 'doer' of the action, the verb is in the active voice. If the subject is the receiver of the action, the verb is in the passive voice. Box 5.1 shows a change from passive to active.

Box 5.1

> The selection of this operation is made automatically by the software if there is no intervention by the operator.
> Unless the operator intervenes, the software selects this function automatically.

Passive constructions are weak, in that the subject is acted upon instead of performing the action. With passive constructions, there is a danger of not stating explicitly who or what performs the action. This can lead to ambiguity and vagueness. Passive constructions usually require more words. Here are two suggestions to help you identify the passive tense, and change it to the active.

Ask of each sentence: 'Where is the action?' If the verb in the sentence is a passive verb, look for an active verb to replace it.

Look for an infinitive immediately after the passive verb. Change the infinitive to an active verb (see Box 5.2).

Box 5.2

> A READ statement is used to assign to the listed variables those values which are obtained from a DATA statement.
> A READ statement assigns the values obtained from a DATA statement to the listed variables.

5.2.2   Using the active voice

When writing instructions, use the active voice. Some writers claim to use the passive voice to lend an air of calmness and professionalism to an otherwise lightweight document. In fact, the passive voice can prevent communication and reduce clarity. Box 5.3 is an example of difference between passive and active when writing instructions.

Box 5.3

> The program can be started by double-clicking on the NITRAM icon.
> Double-click on the NITRAM icon to start the program.

5.2.3   Using the passive voice

The passive voice can be useful for explanations. But make sure that the reader is left in no doubt as to what you mean, as the passive voice can change the stress in a sentence. There are also times when the passive construction cannot be changed to active, as in the sentence 'If the condition is satisfied, control passes to the subroutine'. This sentence must remain passive, since it describes something that happens, not something that the reader must or can do.

Use the passive tense if you want to stress the receiver and take the emphasis off the doer, or if the doer of the action is unknown or unimportant. Do not try to eliminate the passive, but try to restrict its use. The examples in Box 5.4 are more effective in the passive.

<table>
<tr><td>

The sixteen bits of each word are numbered 0 to 15. (The doer is unimportant.)

The input and output units are both shown in Figure 2: in many cases the same device acts as both an input and an output unit. (The emphasis is on the receiver: the doer is unimportant.)

The address of the File Control Block is put on the next free location on the stack. (The doer is unimportant.)

</td><td>

Box 5.4

</td></tr>
</table>

5.3   Clarity

The objective of technical writing is clear, accurate, and concise communication. It is not enough that your book is accurate and at the right level of detail: it must also be easy to follow. If what you have written is clear and easy to understand, you have achieved your goal.

If your writing is not clear, the reader may waste time on unproductive attempts to use the product. This leads to a sense of frustration. Eventually, the reader may put your book aside, and decide to learn by experiment.

When writing your book, always try to put yourself in the place of your reader. Ask yourself the questions 'What will the reader do next?' 'What errors can occur?' 'How do you stop?' and 'What happens if . . . ?' Make sure that your book answers these questions, and try to anticipate all the possible actions and mistakes that the reader might make.

There is a simple rule concerning clarity: never give an incomplete account of what the reader has to do. It is always better to give too much detail than too little. You must also keep the 'What if . . . ?' question in mind. When describing a procedure, never leave the reader thinking 'Yes, but . . . ' or 'I wonder what . . . '.

When describing a particular subject, try to give a complete account of it in one place. Referring the reader to somewhere else, especially in 'How to use . . . ' books, can cause confusion and worry.

The feature of style which has the greatest effect on clarity is simplicity. Technical writing can be made almost as precise as mathematics if it is kept simple. Many books are translated. Others are used in their original English by people whose first language is not English. This means that simplicity is even more important. Follow the rules given here.

Avoid compound sentences, especially those which use 'which' and 'that' too often. It may not always be clear what the 'which' or 'that' is referring to. The following sections cover other aspects of keeping your writing clear.

5.4   Controlled English

5.4.1   *What is 'Controlled English'?*

Controlled English, sometimes called 'Global English', is a predefined sub-set of English for use in documentation. As far as I know, there is no international standard for Controlled English for software manuals, but many companies have their own standard.

Using Controlled English means that you can communicate effectively everything that you need to say, using a vocabulary of perhaps less than 8,000 words. This is because most of the words in the set have a fixed meaning, and you may not use another word in their place. At first sight, many writers think that this will be restrictive, and will not allow them to be as creative as they would like. But, having used it myself on a few occasions, I have found this is not the case. As a writer, you must always keep in mind that your job is to communicate information clearly and accurately, and that any tool or standard that helps this process must be worth using.

Some of the advantages of Controlled English are:

- Easier understanding of documents by non-English speakers
- The possibility to use style and spelling checkers that are adapted to the particular language set
- Lower translation costs, as translation can be automated to a large extent
- Standard word usage leads to improved customer acceptance
- Easier adaptation to specific standards such as those used by the MoD or the Department of Defence.

5.4.2   *The basic rules*

The main rules in any Controlled English set are as follows.

- Use only one word to convey a given meaning. In other words, do not use 'start', 'begin', 'activate', 'launch', and 'run' to mean starting a program. Choose one and use it consistently (see Box 5.5).
- Use each word as only one part of speech. Do not use the same word as a noun and as an adjective. For example, do not use 'open' to mean the action of opening a window on a screen, and as a description of the active window.
- Use only British or American English, but do not mix them. For example, use 'causes' or 'triggers', but not both.
- Use words which come from wide roots, rather than only Latin-based languages. For example, use 'get' rather than 'obtain', and 'purpose' rather than 'intention'.
- Use verb and noun combinations rather than having to add another word to

the set. For example, use 'make sure' rather than 'ensure' and 'take off' rather than 'remove'.

- Restrict yourself to three tenses: simple present, simple past, and simple future.
- Use only four types of sentence; statements, instructions, conditional statements, and questions.
- Use questions only in trouble-shooting manuals, and occasionally in instructions for devices.

<table>
<tr><td>

Examples of single-word usage
recover (v) use for: Keep, Get back, Remove
reduce (v) use for: Decrease
remain (v) use for: Stay
remedy (v) use for: Repair, Make correct

</td><td>

Box 5.5

</td></tr>
</table>

5.5   Sentence length

5.5.1   Introduction

Your book must not consist entirely of short, dry statements of fact. On the other hand, if you write nothing but one long sentence after another, you will irritate your reader. Avoid both extremes: a natural variation in sentence length will hold the reader's interest and increase the clarity of the writing.

Nevertheless, do not use a long word where a short one will do. Long words lead to long sentences, which get even longer when they are translated. Even the expression 'vending cups' (plastic beakers in automatic coffee machines) becomes five words in French. Long sentences can result in a complicated structure, and what you are trying to say may become distorted or unclear. On the other hand, a succession of too short sentences breaks up the flow of information from you to the reader.

Ideally, a sentence should be an easily understandable unit of information. The more ideas you try to express in one sentence, the harder it is for the reader to absorb what you are trying to say. Even if your readers are already familiar with some of the subject matter, they will still appreciate easily digested units of information.

Many books are translated. Simple, clear sentences are easier to translate, and there is less chance for the meaning to become distorted during translation. Follow the rules given below.

- Use short simple sentences.
- Try to keep to between 13 and 21 words per sentence. In spite of what many books say, surveys show that sentences with an average length of 9 words are less legible than those with a 13-word average.
- Remove unnecessary words, but avoid 'telegraphese'. In the 'telegraphese' style the principle of omitting superfluous words is carried to extremes. Any

word not contributing directly to the meaning is omitted, even at the expense of grammar and sentence structure. This style is unsuitable for the majority of applications, but has its place in summaries and checklists.

Box 5.6 shows an example of a long sentence, with a suggested improvement.

Box 5.6

> *Example*
> You can use TM-BASIC to check that a value entered is within a certain range, to compare data against a value in another data variable, to perform check-digit calculations, or to perform other arithmetic and logical operations.
> *Improvement*
> You can use TM-BASIC to:
>
> - Check that a value entered is within a certain range
> - Compare data against a value in another data variable
> - Perform check-digit calculations
> - Perform other arithmetic and logical operations.

Note the use of a list in Box 5.6. You can find more information about using lists in Chapter 4.

The briefest of technical notes can communicate effectively to well-qualified individuals. In the computer industry many people are well informed in certain areas and unpredictably ignorant in others. This means that you must assume that your reader has a level of understanding lower than the ideal. But remember that your readers are intelligent and generally willing to learn. Present your ideas in a straightforward way, avoiding flattery and condescension.

5.5.2 *Redundancy and padding*

These are two more causes of long sentences. The three main reasons for redundancy and padding in technical manuals are unclear thinking, the desire to produce an apparently large volume of work, and unwillingness to rewrite.

1. *Unclear thinking*

If you do not fully understand the subject you are describing, you are often unable to think about it properly. Sometimes this results in writers skirting around the points they do not understand. If you find this happening to you, ask for technical help.

2. *The desire to produce a large volume of work*

Some writers feel that their ability is judged by the number of pages they produce. This can result in them doing one or more of the following:

- Putting more information into a book than the reader actually needs, and in some cases irrelevant information.
- Making the same point more than once in different ways, thereby confusing the reader, who thinks that there are several points being made, when there is only one.
- Showing off their knowledge of the subject by describing everything they know on it, rather than describing what the reader needs to know.

3. *Unwillingness to rewrite*

If you reread your work and it does not fully describe the point you are trying to make, do not be tempted to add information instead of rewriting what exists. If you have to read something a number of times before you understand it, it needs rewriting.

5.6 Pompous style

The result of a pompous style is that readers think they are having trouble with the subject, when in fact they are just having trouble with the vocabulary. Pompous style can also be the result of long sentences, or the overuse of jargon and technical terms. Do not assume that your readers will know what a word means just because you do. Express yourself in the simplest way. Use words of one syllable rather than words of many syllables (see Box 5.7).

<table>
<tr><td>

Example
Due to the upcoming project submission to support the system upgrade as well as the introduction of the new product, it is becoming eminent to identify all capital requirements for this process. Your input is important for the resolution of this issue.
Improvement
Please supply your capital requirements for the future support of the system upgrade and the new product.

</td><td>

Box 5.7

</td></tr>
</table>

5.7 Jargon and technical terms

5.7.1 *Jargon*

Manuals seem unable to escape jargon because computers fascinate those who work around them, and because the people who write about computers are not afraid of computers or the jargon that goes with them. Eliminating jargon from software manuals is becoming more important as more people use computers. The new users are generally experts in a particular business, but are uninterested in computers except as tools for getting the job done faster and more easily. For these people, jargon is both a hindrance and an irritation. Jargon can be effective shorthand for those who understand it, but it is a barrier to the uninitiated.

Until now, manual writers have tried three solutions, with varying success:

- Providing glossaries of the technical terms in brackets in the text.
- Providing a glossary of terms, usually at the end of the manual.
- Expressing the ideas in other words.

Each of these solutions helps the new reader, but each also has drawbacks. The best solution will come when a new generation of software is itself free of jargon, which I doubt will ever happen. It is a tendency of specialist groups to develop jargon, consisting of coined words and misused phrases which do not always mean the same thing to all readers. This means that you must avoid using jargon in your book as much as possible. If you need to use a technical term, define it (if possible without the use of further jargon in the explanation), and include it in the glossary. If you can avoid using a technical term, do so. The Bibliography at the end of this book includes some reference books that you may find useful for finding definitions of technical terms, so that you do not have to make them up yourself.

Of course, you cannot explain a subject to a novice without using some technical terms or jargon, but their use should be sensibly controlled. Never assume knowledge on the reader's part. Stay aware of the words you are using: it is very easy to use technical terms without noticing, simply because they are the ones you yourself are familiar with.

The computer world is full of jargon. But that does not necessarily mean that it has to appear in the books as well. If you find yourself using jargon, stop and consider. Is there anywhere else that the reader will come across the word or phrase? If not, do not use it. Consider using 'Start' instead of 'Initialise', 'Stop' instead of 'Terminate', and so on. One good example from the world of PCs is 'Booting'. If the user will never be faced with this word in screen messages, applications, and so on, then it does not help to use it, even with an explanation.

A lot of jargon can be very worrying, especially for a new user, and should on no account occur in the Preface of a tutorial or introductory book.

If you are working from specifications, and you come across jargon that you think is unnecessary, see if you can influence a change in the software. For example, if the specification says that the screen heading is 'Primary Function Selection Screen', do not just copy it: suggest that it is changed to 'Main Menu'.

5.7.2   Technical terms

You should use technical terms to give precision, when ordinary language has carried the reader as far as it can. Many concepts, even in the world of computing, can be expressed in everyday English.

If you need to use a technical term, define it and include it in the glossary. If you can avoid using a technical term, do so. Explain any term as you use it for the first time, and then use the term precisely. Wherever possible, refer to a dictionary or glossary for your definition, rather than making up one yourself.

5.8   Variety and inconsistency

Although you should try to use some variety in your writing, beware of using synonyms of technical terms for the sake of variety. Your reader will inevitably look for a distinction where there is none. Similarly, while varying your style, do not introduce inconsistencies. This applies not only to the writing itself, but also to the presentation. Inconsistency of tables or figures can lead to confusion.

5.9   Numbers

This section describes how to write numbers in manuals, including:

- Numbers in text
- Chapter, section, page, and part numbers
- Decimals
- Numbers associated with a unit
- Dates
- Times
- Telephone numbers.

5.9.1   Numbers in text

Write all numbers from zero to twenty as one word. Write the numbers thirty, forty, fifty, sixty, seventy, eighty, and ninety as one word as well. Use hyphens to separate the tens and units of numbers twenty-one to twenty-nine and similar multiples.

Write numbers above ninety-nine in Arabic numbers, for example 100 rather than 'one hundred' and 6,251 rather than six thousand, two hundred and fifty-one. For very large numbers, use commas as separators for the thousandfolds, for example: 10,000,000. One exception to the rule about numbers above 99, however, is when a sentence starts with a number: then you must write the number in words.

Never split a number across two lines, even if there is a natural line break at a hyphen.

Avoid the terms billion, milliard, trillion, and so on, because the exact meanings of these terms differ between English-speaking nations.

5.9.2   Chapter, section, page, and part numbers

Unless your standards state otherwise, always write chapter, section, page, and part numbers in Arabic numerals (see Box 5.8).

<table><tr><td>Box 5.8</td><td>

For more information, see Chapter 4.
The manual can be ordered quoting part number 5129 926631

</td></tr></table>

5.9.3 Decimals

When expressing a number involving a decimal point, use a full stop to represent the point: for example, 24.77 degrees.

Although some countries use the comma as the decimal point and the full stop as the thousands separator, I assume that you are writing in English. If your manual is later translated, it is up to the translator to change these if necessary.

5.9.4 Numbers associated with a unit

When you write the unit in full, leave a space between the number and the unit. This is also the case where a multiplication factor is used. Do not split the number and the units over two lines. If you use an abbreviation for the unit, do not leave a space between the number and the unit (see Box 5.9).

<table><tr><td>Box 5.9</td><td>

This machine uses a 2000 watt motor.
Do not use a bulb stronger than 60W.
The program needs 256 Kbytes of disk space.
The buffer must be at least 256Kb in length.

</td></tr></table>

Note the use of 'Kbytes' and 'Kb' in Box 5.9. The term K used in computing is not a unit but a multiplication factor meaning 2^{10}. It makes as much sense to write of a memory of 256K as to say an apple weighs five. Use Kbytes and Mbytes, not K and M.

If using a space could lead to ambiguity, use a hyphen instead (see Box 5.10). The hyphen makes it clear that the writer means motors rated at 2kW, and not 2000 motors rated at 1 watt each.

<table><tr><td>Box 5.10</td><td>

The next version will use 2000-watt motors.

</td></tr></table>

5.9.5 Dates

To describe a specific day in a month, use the ordinal number, the word 'of', and then the month, starting with a capital letter (see Box 5.11). If you include the year in a date, put a comma between the month and the year, as in 'the 12th of January, 1988', for example.

<table><tr><td>Box 5.11</td><td>

April Fool's day is celebrated on the 1st of April.

</td></tr></table>

5.9.6 *Times*

Use digits to write times, regardless of whether you choose to use 'am' and 'pm' or the 24-hour clock representation. The following two sentences mean the same thing:

The system closed down at 4.00 pm.
The system closed down at 16:00 hours.

5.9.7 *Telephone numbers*

Telephone numbers are difficult to standardise, because different countries use different standards. One standard in general use in Europe is as follows:

+country-code area-code line-number (extension-number)

The + indicates that international dialling must be used (the actual code varies from one country to another). Any elements except line-number can be omitted, but obviously if country-code is given, the area-code cannot be omitted. Note that the area-code must often include a leading zero if the country-code is omitted (see Box 5.12).

1 4327 2196 and + 33 1 4327 2196 are the same number, in Paris, France, where the first is the local convention, and the second is the European convention.

Box 5.12

5.10   Highlighting

5.10.1 *Introduction*

I use the term 'highlighting' to cover the use of bold, italic, and underlined text. You may well have your own or a company standard to work to. But I have seen standards which, when applied, only result in clutter and confusion on the page. The main thing to remember about highlighting is to use it sparingly, and consistently. The following sections describe the rules I try to apply myself, and that I have used successfully in several companies.

5.10.1 *Bold*

Use bold for:

- Main section headings
- Subsection headings
- Figure and table titles
- Emphasis
- Commands
- File and directory names.

Box 5.13 gives some examples of the last three categories.

Box 5.13

> Note that in this case the file is **not** saved.
> Use the **dfree** command to find out how much disk space is available.
> Copy the files **wz.bat** and **wz.exe** to the **system** directory on your hard disk.

5.10.2   Italics

Use italics for:

- References to other manuals
- Symbolic names
- Variables in command syntax
- Long pieces of user input.

We saw the first of these categories earlier in this chapter. Box 5.14 gives some examples of the others.

Box 5.14

> The file *filename* cannot be found. This means that the file is not in the current directory.
> Enter the command **dfree** *disk-letter*: where *disk-letter* is C or D.
> Type the following text: *This is to inform you that we have received your order, and that it will be dealt with without delay.*

5.10.3   Underlining

Do not use underlining for emphasis. Underlined text is more difficult to read than ordinary, bold, or italic text.

5.11   Capitalisation

5.11.1   Introduction

Use initial capitals to denote a proper noun or to focus the reader's attention on a particular word (for example, Chapter, Figure, or Table). Use capitals elsewhere according to the rules of English grammar.

Above all, be consistent. If a term or word has an initial capital, each occurrence of the term or word throughout the book must be the same.

When describing commands, filenames, directories, path names, and programming statements, use upper and lower case as dictated by the operating system or programming language.

Use a leading capital for proprietary names of hardware or software, except where the owner uses another convention. For example, MS-DOS must always be in all capitals, and WordPerfect has an initial capital and a capital P.

5.11.2   All capitals

Use all capitals for:

- Chapter and appendix titles (except in references)
- Section headings
- Figure and table titles
- Acronyms such as MOS, RAM, ROM, and so on, except where customarily spelt otherwise
- Logical operators (for example: AND, OR, NOT)
- Entries in the glossary.

5.11.3   All lower case

Use all lower case for:

- Sub-entries in an index (except where convention dictates otherwise)
- Generic names of software and hardware (for example: system disk, operating system, compiler)
- Names of system devices and mechanisms (for example: password, menu)
- Names of system procedures and operations (for example: editing, file handling)
- Descriptive names of functions, commands, and modes (for example: filing function, activation command, multi-user mode)
- Names of variables (for example: filename, string, volume-id)
- Symbolic names.

5.11.4   Leading capitals

Use a leading capital for:

- Subsection headings
- References to sections in text
- All heading entries in the Table of Contents
- Main entries in an index
- Job titles ('System Administrator')
- Column headings in tables
- Names of screen fields and menu items.

Use a leading capital on significant words for:

- References to manual titles
- References to chapter and appendix titles
- References to figure and table titles.

5.12   Colloquialisms and slang

5.12.1   Colloquialisms

Avoid colloquialisms: they may sound friendly in English, but the translator or reader may never have heard of them. The same goes for idiomatic expressions which may not have an equivalent in another language. What do I mean by a colloquialism? Take the phrase 'the biggest ever pools win', for example. While this means something to a British audience, what do you think a Mexican will make of it?

Of course, a good translator can turn such a phrase into one that makes sense in the target language. But you never know who is going to be reading your book in its original English, and they may be of a different nationality.

5.12.2   Slang

You should also avoid slang, for the same reasons as those given for colloquialisms. By slang I mean expressions such as 'up the creek' and 'give it a whirl'.

5.13   Humour

Once you are a skilled and experienced writer writing for a known audience, you may be able to increase your impact by the careful use of humour. In my view, however, humour has no place in technical writing. The purpose of a technical book is not entertainment, but communication. Moreover, sense of humour varies unpredictably from individual to individual and from country to country. For example, a deputy director-general at the EC Commission in Brussels once said 'If you make an after-dinner speech in the UK, you are heavily criticised if you don't make a joke. In France you'll be criticised if you do. They'll say, he's a clown, a lightweight, especially a politician'. What may appear amusing to one reader may prove incomprehensible to a second, and offensive to a third.

Some writers say that humour can help to get the reader on your side, especially when you are forced to describe something that may be new to the reader. Here is an example that I came across once. 'Computerniks call this list of numbered descriptions a menu. It works like a menu at a roadside café. If you want scrambled eggs with hash brown potatoes, toast, jelly and coffee, you can just say "I'll have a number 5".' My view of this is that, in the first place, the word 'computerniks' is off-putting, and, in the second place, the writer is going way over the top in his attempt at humour. In this case, that of explaining a menu, it should be adequate just to describe how to choose something, and introduce the term 'menu'.

To give you another example from a software manual I read recently, part of the disclaimer reads 'By using the product you accept said product in its' [sic] current state of development. Contents may settle. May be made in one or more EEC countries. 100% pure wool. This is NOT an admission of guilt. Cottons only!' I personally find this completely 'un-funny'. I have paid good money for a serious software product, and this is what I find in the manual. If the product developers have the same sense of humour as the authors, what can I expect from the product?

Another example, this time from a manual written in Canada. At the beginning of the tutorial chapter I came across the sentence 'Pull up a screen and follow along'.

Remember that not only do some people really dislike this sort of thing, but that some are actively put off by it, and will not be prepared to take your manual seriously. This means that they will not take you as the author seriously either. In addition, it only takes a translator having a bad day to turn this sort of humour into complete nonsense in a foreign-language version of your book.

5.14   Using 'he' or 'she'

If you address your reader directly, you will normally avoid the problem of using 'he' or 'she'. The few places left where you may apparently need to make this choice can often be solved by simply rewriting, as shown in Box 5.15.

If this happens, tell your system administrator. He will have to reset your password before you can log in again. If this happens, ask your system administrator to reset your password, and then log in again.

Box 5.15

You can also replace 'him' by 'they' in some circumstances, and still make your meaning clear (Box 5.16).

Change the workstation database to include the new workstation, and ask him to log in again. Change the workstation database to include the new workstation, and ask them to log in again.

Box 5.16

5.15   Using 'must', 'should', 'can', and 'may'

5.15.1   'Must' and 'should'

The difference between 'must' and 'should' is very important in software documentation. 'Must' means that the action is obligatory: 'should' means that it is advisable. If the user must do something, say so. If you are advising them, then avoid the word 'should', and use a phrase such as 'It is recommended that . . . '. Even your readers might take 'should' to mean obligatory.

5.15.2   'Can' and 'may'

There is also a distinction between 'can' and 'may'. 'Can' implies capability: 'may' is a vague word and can be interpreted as meaning permission or possibility.

5.16   Acronyms and abbreviations

5.16.1   Introduction

An acronym is an abbreviation, usually made up of the first letter (or letters) of the significant words of the full name or description. Examples are Radar (RAdio Detection And Ranging) and Laser (Light Amplification by Stimulated Emission of Radiation). If the abbreviation is not pronounceable as a word (SPM, for example), it is strictly speaking not an acronym. However, for the purposes of this book, I class acronyms as any abbreviations formed according to the rules stated above.

Abbreviations and contractions are shortened versions of words, formed through the omission of some letters. Examples are Mr for Mister, Prof. for Professor, Inc. for Incorporated, Ltd for Limited, and so on.

5.16.2   Acronyms

The first time you use an acronym, other than those which are now part of everyday speech (such as radar), give the full term first with the acronym after it in parentheses (see Box 5.17).

Box 5.17

> The Central Processing Unit (CPU) is the part ...

Note that some acronyms are always in capitals (COBOL, for example) and some are all in lower case (laser). You must choose the appropriate form, but generally they are all capitals, with no full stops in between.

It does no harm to repeat the full term here and there to remind the reader especially if the acronym appears only at infrequent intervals throughout the book.

Note that the plural form of an acronym is made by adding 's'. Do not use an apostrophe. Thus the plural of NCO is NCOs and that of PC is PCs.

Never assume that your reader understands abbreviations. To some people PC means Personal Computer, to others Program Counter, and to others Police Constable or Privy Councillor. Make sure you state what you mean.

This principle should really be extended to terms such as Random Access Memory (RAM) and Read Only Memory (ROM). When referring to an area of read only memory, it is best to use the words 'read only memory'. Use RAM and ROM only to refer to certain types of chip.

In the case of acronyms which are also the names of software packages, there is no need to explain the acronym. The reader will accept what you write as the name.

5.16.3   Abbreviations

Use only known abbreviations: do not make up your own. You may laugh, but I have seen it done. If the last letter of the abbreviation is the last letter of the original word, do not follow it with a full stop. If the last letter is not the last letter of the word, follow it with a full stop (Co. for company, for example).

In general, try to avoid abbreviations, and use them only in figures and tables where space is limited. Write place names, dates and times, months, personal names, and titles in full, unless your company or client prefers an abbreviated form. For example, you should always write the word 'January' in full in normal text. 'JAN' or 'Jan' is permissible in a figure or table, as it is a commonly accepted abbreviation. Note that in this case, it is normal practice to omit the full stop.

Avoid using common abbreviations that were originally Latin, such as *etc.*, *idem, i.e.*, and *e.g.*. Of course, it may not always be possible to avoid using them, but try to use 'and so on', 'the same as', 'that is to say', and 'for example' instead. If you have to use *etc.*, please remember that one occurrence is enough: writing *etc., etc.* is overkill and meaningless.

5.17 Punctuation

5.17.1 Introduction

Most written languages use punctuation rules which make the writing easier to read, and help to avoid ambiguity. This section is not intended to be a complete course in how to punctuate, but I am trying here to draw some points to your attention that many writers get wrong, or do not understand. There are many excellent books on punctuation, and if there isn't one on your bookshelf right at this moment, stop reading, and go out and buy one. The Bibliography at the end of this book lists some of the ones that I find useful.

5.17.2 Full stop

Always use a full stop at the end of a sentence. Do not use a full stop after a heading.

5.17.3 Ellipsis

The ellipsis has three uses.

- To indicate something missing from a quotation, as in 'A magnificent book ... I couldn't put it down.' It is unlikely that you will need to use the ellipsis in this way when writing software manuals.
- To show that something can be repeated in a syntax description (see User input). Whether you use it or not depends on the type of language or commands you are describing.
- To show that a section of a program listing, or other long piece of text, has been omitted.

5.17.4 Colon

The function of the colon is '... delivering the goods that have been invoiced in the preceding words' (Fowler's *A Dictionary of Modern English Usage*). It

is connected to the ideas 'namely', 'as follows', or 'because', even if those words
are not present in the sentence (see Box 5.18).

Box 5.18

> You can use this package to manage all the user parameters: user-
> ids, login names, and passwords.
> Take great care when cleaning the printhead: solvent in contact
> with the toner may cause the printer to explode.

You can also use a colon to separate two closely connected, but contrasting,
clauses (see Box 5.19).

Box 5.19

> This option is only available when you have already saved the
> password file: otherwise you must use the system management
> utility.

5.17.5 Semicolon

Use a semicolon to separate two clauses which are closely connected and which
would result in 'bittiness' if written separately (see Box 5.20).

Box 5.20

> 'Secretarial is the adjective corresponding to secretary; secretariat
> is the official . . . establishment of a secretary' (Partridge's *Usage
> and Abusage*).

You should try to avoid using a semicolon in sentences where a conjunction
such as 'and' or 'or' will make the meaning clearer or the construction smoother.

5.17.6 Comma

Use commas, in pairs or combined with another stop, to separate subordinate
clauses (see Box 5.21). In my experience, people are divided on whether or not
to use a comma to separate the last item in a series, as in Box 5.22. This is because
teachers of English used to say that it was not necessary, although in modern
English usage, it is becoming the norm.

Box 5.21

> The Archive Manager, which you can start from the File Menu,
> enables you to search for any documents in the archive.

Box 5.22

> You can use the File Manager to copy, find, and delete files.

In Box 5.22 it is clear that you must use a comma instead of repeating the word
'and', as otherwise the last phrase would read 'find and delete files', and this
obviously is not the correct meaning. My advice is always to use a comma in
this sort of situation: at least you know that your meaning will be clear.

5.17.7 *Hyphen*

Use hyphens to combine otherwise independent words to prevent a phrase
appearing absurd or difficult to read. Do not leave a space at either side of the
hyphen, as I have seen in many documents: this has a completely different use,
as explained below. Box 5.23 shows a sentence in which the wording leads the
brain to expect a different construction, and therefore confuses the reader. The
second sentence shows how you can improve it by using a hyphen.

When business financed projects in the area have been developed . . . When business-financed projects in the area have been developed . . .	**Box 5.23**

Depending on the standards that you have to follow, you may also be able to
use the hyphen to separate a sub-clause in a sentence, as in Box 5.24.

The network addresses — which are specified during the installation phase — cannot be changed.	**Box 5.24**

I personally feel that placing the sub-clause in brackets, or between commas,
is equally meaningful, but there are certainly software manuals around which
use the hyphen in this way. Most of the manuals I have seen that use this convention
have been written by non-English writers, and it may well be that other languages
use this convention more than English. One American writer put it this way: 'Use
commas . . . when you want to slip something in without making a big deal. Use
parentheses . . . when you want to play down the insertion. Use dashes . . . when
you want to grab the reader by the throat.'

5.17.8 *Apostrophe*

The apostrophe (') implies 'belonging to'. The phrase 'Martyn's book' shows
that the book belongs to Martyn. In the case of plural ownership, the apostrophe
must follow the owners. Thus, 'a book's cover' is singular, but 'the books' covers'
is plural.

All pronouns except 'one' do not use an apostrophe. This means that 'hers',
'yours', 'his', 'theirs', and 'its' are written without one, and 'one's' has an
apostrophe. Using an apostrophe in 'its' (it's) is used only for the abbreviation
of 'it is'.

Please remember that plurals of acronyms such as PC do not have an apostrophe,
for example 'Up to 16 PCs can be connected'. It is becoming the fashion to write
'PC's' and 'LAN's' for the plural, but it is completely unnecessary. To give you
an example of what can happen when someone does not understand how to use
an apostrophe, let me quote the text that appeared on a sign outside a bus station
in Sevenoaks while I was writing this book: 'BUSE'S ONLY'!

5.17.9 *Quotation marks*

My personal recommendation for using quotation marks is as follows (although some publishers have a different standard). Only use double quotation marks for genuine quotations. Use the double form (" ") to contain the quotation, and the single form (' ') for quotations within a quotation (see Box 5.25).

Box 5.25

> Mr Travers said "I am sure you are all familiar with the words 'Et tu, Brute' from Shakespeare's *Julius Caesar*".

You can also use the single quotation marks when introducing a term for the first time, as in Box 5.26.

Box 5.26

> This structure is known as an 'organisational unit'.

Of course, it is possible that your standards state that you should use italic or bold type for this purpose. But in many companies, the use of italic or bold is restricted. This is for a very good reason: if the reader is faced with a lot of bold or italic text in a paragraph, his eye is drawn to that text, and he may not read every word. Your job is to make sure that every word counts, and that your reader does read every word.

Many writers use the single quotation mark to highlight names of menus, input fields, and so on, in tutorial manuals. In my opinion, you should only do this if not doing so would make the meaning unclear (see Box 5.27).

Box 5.27

> Choose the Delete option from the File menu.
> Choose the 'Option' option from the File menu.

In the second case in Box 5.27, the quotation marks are necessary to enable the reader to understand the instruction at first reading.

5.17.10 *Parentheses*

Make sure that parentheses always appear in pairs. You would be surprised to see how many books there are where the writer has forgotten the closing parenthesis here and there. Normally you do not need to combine them with any other punctuation. You should use them when you want to add a short remark to the reader without interrupting the flow of the sentence (see Box 5.28). Sometimes you may be able to use hyphens instead (see Hyphen, above).

Box 5.28

> The network addresses (which are specified during installation) cannot be changed.

5.17.11   Exclamation marks and question marks

You should use these only in genuine exclamations and questions, respectively. In most cases, you will probably only come across exclamation marks when documenting error messages, such as 'File not found!'. In these cases, go to your developers, and insist that they remove the exclamation mark from the message text. Users can read the message text and understand it without the exclamation mark screaming at them from the screen.

As far as question marks are concerned, only use them when you are genuinely asking the reader a question. This is only likely when you are writing a flowchart or decision table.

5.18   Summary

This chapter has concentrated on the style of writing, including such things as sentence length, correct use of tense, and punctuation. Using this information together with what has gone before should make your book clear, well-written, and understandable.

But there are other ways of explaining things, using graphics such as tables and figures. The next chapter looks at these possibilities.

6   Graphic elements

'One picture is worth ten thousand words'

Frederick R. Barnard, in *Printer's Ink*

6.1 Introduction

Illustrations, if used properly, can contribute greatly to the effectiveness of a book. An illustration can shorten and simplify the text it supports. If you think an illustration will help your reader to understand your book more easily, use one. There are a number of different types of illustrations that you can use, such as:

- Tables
- Railroad diagrams
- Graphs
- Flow charts
- Alpha key diagrams
- Drawings and line diagrams
- Photographs.

6.2 Tables

A table provides a quick method of looking up related information that a reader will refer to a number of times. A table should make the information easier to find, understand, and use. Indeed, a bank in America was able to reduce more than 14 pages of instructions to their cashiers to a single look-up table that fitted on an A4 sheet of paper.

When deciding whether to use a table, consider the following points.

- How often will a reader want to refer to the table?
- What information will the reader want to extract from the table?
- What is the reader's point of entry into the table?

If a reader will read the book once only, then any tables will also be read once only. In this case a table may not be the best way of presenting that information.

Give all your tables titles which are as short and precise as possible. Depending on your standards, you may also number tables

Table 6.1 Set 1 DIP switches
Note: Switch 1-3 is not used. Leave it off

	1	2	4	5	6	7	8
Floppy drive A:							
360KB	ON						
1.2MB	OFF						
Coprocessor							
Installed		OFF					
Not installed		ON					
Internal parallel interface							
Primary			OFF				
Secondary			ON				
Monitor type							
Disable internal video				ON	ON		
Colour (40 x 25)				OFF	ON		
Colour (80 x 25)				ON	OFF		
Monochrome				OFF	OFF		
Number of floppy drives							
One						ON	ON
Two						OFF	ON

Try to make sure that a table is not separated from the text to which it relates by a page turn. If at all possible the table should appear on the same double-page spread as the relevant text. If the table is referred to a number of times, then this rule applies only to the first reference.

When you refer to a table within the text, use both the number of the table and the title, for example 'see Table 12, Overview of the file control mechanism'.

Once you have made your table, get someone else to look at it. Many writers make tables that they understand, but that confuse their readers. Consider the (genuine) example of a decision table in Table 6.1, and decide what is wrong with it.

What is wrong with this table? To start with, it has blank entries in it. At first, this seems to be an oversight of some sort, but on closer inspection we can see that the blank entries actually relate to headings. However, the headings themselves are not highlighted in any way.

In addition, although the text above the table mentions Switch 1-3, it does not appear in the table, and the reader may well miss the fact that it must be off. Table 6.2 is an example of the same information, laid out in a more understandable way.

I realise that this is a difficult example to solve, on account of the fact that some switches are only used in combination with others. But as long as you see the original problem, and agree that my proposal is an improvement, that is all that matters here.

The sequence of the columns in a table is very important. Since the reader naturally reads from left to right, the entrance point to the information must be at the left. Consider Table 6.3, which is also part of a genuine one.

At first sight, this appears to be a well laid-out table, until you know the manual

Table 6.2

Switch	Condition	On/Off
1	Floppy drive A: 360Kb	ON
	Floppy drive A: 1.2Mb	OFF
2	Coprocessor installed	OFF
	No copressor installed	ON
3	NOT USED (must be Off)	OFF
4	Primary internal parallel interface	OFF
	Secondary parallel interface	ON
5 and 6	Disable monitor internal video	Both ON
	Colour (40 × 25)	5 OFF, 6 ON
	Colour (80 × 25)	5 ON, 6 OFF
	Monochrome	Both OFF
7 and 8	One floppy drive	Both ON
	Two floppy drives	7 Off, 8 ON

Table 6.3 XTREE FILE commands

Command	Key	Description
Attrib	**A**	Displays a file's attributes for verification or change: attributes include read-only, hidden, system and archive
	Ctrl A	Changes attributes of all tagged files
Copy	**C**	Copies file at cursor position
	Ctrl C	Copies all tagged files
	Alt C	Copies all tagged files, duplicating directories as necessary
Delete	**D**	Deletes file at cursor position
	Ctrl D	Deletes all tagged files
Execute	**X**	Executes external utility without exiting XTREE
File display	**Alt F**	Changes the format of the display window
Files	**F**	Sets a new file specification in FILE BOX
Log	**L**	Logs onto different disk
Move	**M**	Moves the current file to another directory
	Ctrl M	Moves all tagged files to another directory
Print	**P**	Prints the current file on the printer
	Ctrl P	Prints tagged files on the printer

it was drawn from. What the reader actually wants to look up is how to do something. In other words, he knows the function he wants (listed under 'Description'), but does not know the command or access key. Now you realise that the table is in fact back to front. The description should come first. Table 6.4 is an example of how this table could be improved.

As you can see, I have left out the 'Command' column altogether. This is because it has no relevance to the new table. In the new one, only the actions and the keys are listed, and that is all the user needs.

Table 6.4

Action	Key
Change the attributes of all tagged files	**Ctrl-A**
Change the format of the display window	**Alt-F**
Copy all tagged files	**Ctrl-C**
Copy all tagged files, duplicating directories as necessary	**Alt-C**
Copy the file at the cursor position	**C**
Delete all tagged files	**Ctrl D**
Delete the file at the cursor position	**D**
Display a file's attributes for verification or change: attributes include read-only, hidden, system and archive	**A**
Execute external utility without exiting XTREE	**X**
Log on to a different disk	**L**
Move all tagged files to another directory	**Ctrl-M**
Move the current file to another directory	**M**
Print all tagged files on the printer	**Ctrl-P**
Print the current file on the printer	**P**
Set a new file specification in FILE BOX	**F**

6.3   Railroad diagrams

Railroad diagrams are useful ways of showing how the user reaches a certain point in the software. Figure 6.1 shows a railroad diagram, indicating the structure of menus through which the user must move in order to print the current page of a document. The example shows that the user must first choose 'to Printer' from the Print menu, and then choose 'Current page' from the options offered.

As this example is black and white, I have used bold and a different font to highlight the path through the menus. If you have colour available, it would be more effective to use colour for this. These sorts of diagrams are best used in reference manuals, to give the user a quick view of what he must do. You can also use them in training manuals, to give an overview of the steps you are about to describe. Note that they do not indicate any of the resulting screen contents: they assume that the user will follow the path correctly. In training manuals, it would be best to follow them with numbered steps, and show the resulting menu that appears at each step, so that the users can get visual confirmation that they are following the correct path.

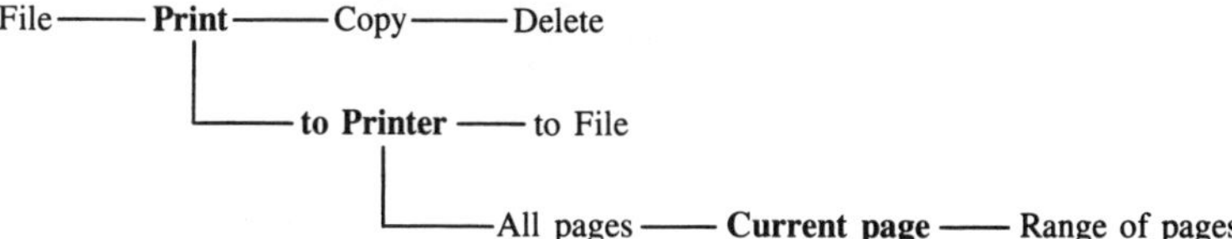

Figure 6.1

6.4   Graphs

There are three basic types of graph that can be useful in software documentation. These are bar graphs, line graphs, and pie charts. The following sections look at each of these.

6.4.1   Bar graphs

Bar graphs provide a quick method for comparing items, where the comparison is more important than the actual values of the items. For example, you might use such a graph to represent a growth pattern, as shown in Figure 6.2. Although this example is in black and white, you may be able to use colour to highlight the actual figures (1991−1993) and the forecast ones (1994−1995).

6.4.2   Line graphs

Line graphs are best suited to showing continuous data. They can be used to provide a detailed method for comparing two or more items. You could use these to show differences in performance, as in Figure 6.3.

Of course, you need to identify the two things you are comparing. You could use dotted or dashed lines, or different colours if colour is available to you. Do not forget to put a key, to show what each type of line or colour means.

6.4.3   Pie charts

Pie charts provide a method for showing the proportions of a whole, for example how much memory is used by different programs. Figure 6.4 is an example of this type of graph.

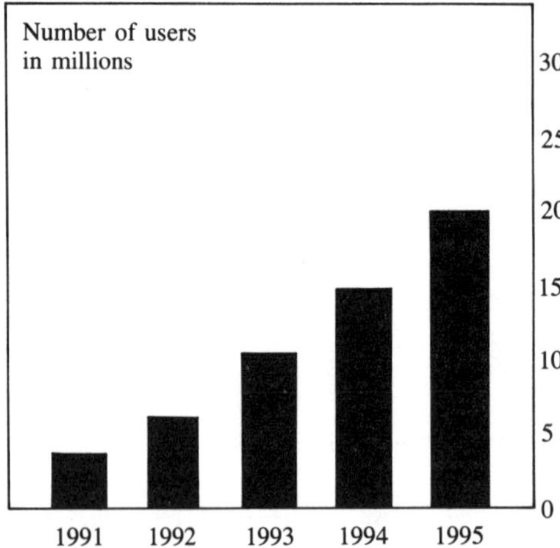

Figure 6.2

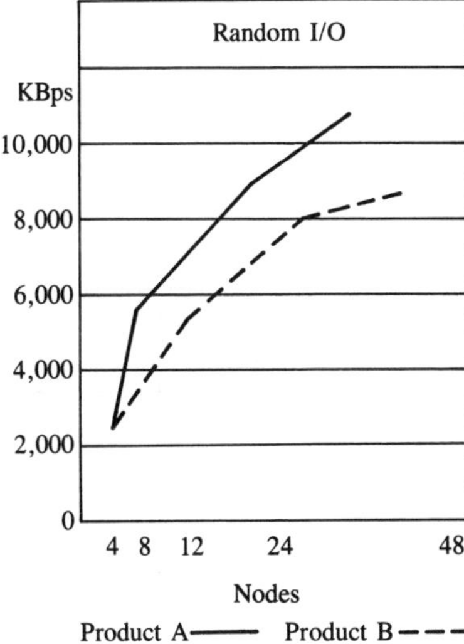

Figure 6.3

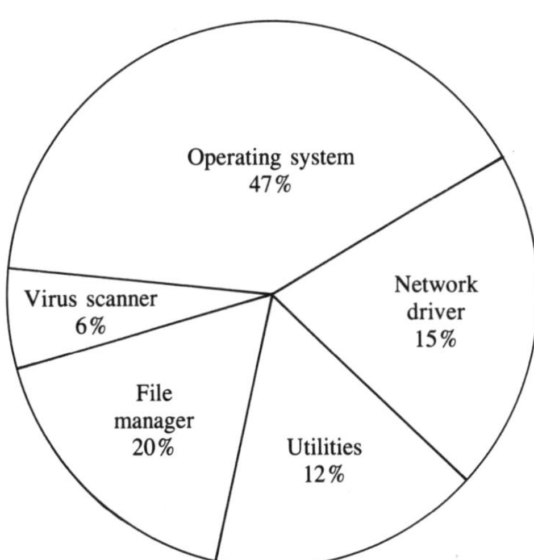

Figure 6.4

You can highlight any particular segment, by using colour, or by showing it as a 'slice', removed slightly from the rest of the pie. Be careful with these sorts of charts: they can introduce apparent distortion, because very small elements tend to look bigger than they actually are. Pie charts containing many small elements are also difficult to read.

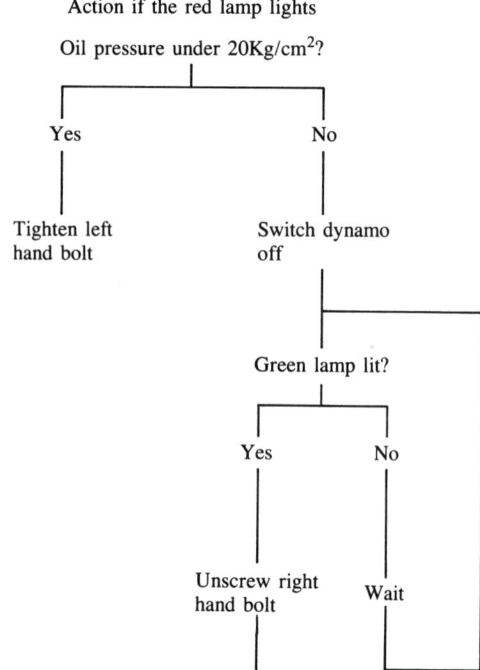

Figure 6.5

6.5   Flow charts

Flow charts are an extremely effective way of showing the basic logic of a program or of a procedure. But not everyone has seen them before: if you think your readers will not have seen them before, make sure that you explain how they are used at the beginning of the book or of the relevant chapter. Figure 6.5 is a small example of a flowchart.

6.6   Alpha key diagrams

Alpha key diagrams are useful when you need to show and label several parts of an illustration. Typical examples of these are the parts of a keyboard or of a dialogue on a screen.

Figure 6.6 is an example of an alpha key diagram, showing the parts of a screen dialogue box, taken from Microsoft Windows.

This type of illustration is best used to introduce a particular view of something to the user, and to explain the terminology being used later in the manual. Very often you see these sorts of pictures in manuals for video recorders and personal organisers, giving an overview of the controls. You could also use them in reference manuals, to give a quick overview.

Do not make them too cluttered, however. If necessary, break the illustration

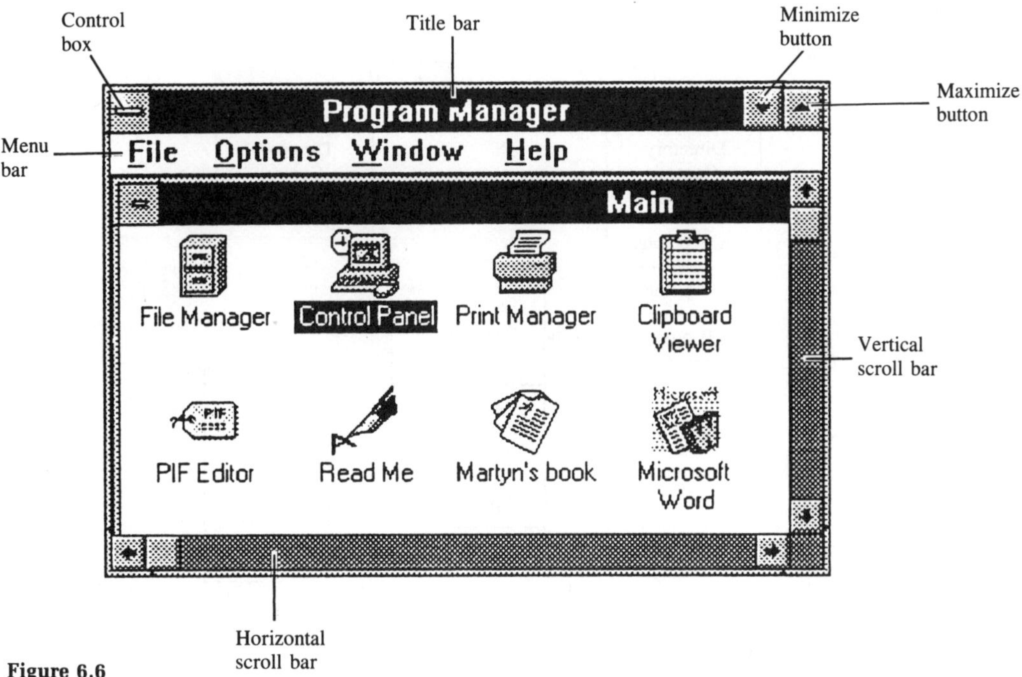

Figure 6.6

into parts, and explain each part separately. If you do this, make sure that the relationship between the parts stays visible to the reader.

6.7   Line diagrams

Line diagrams can be simple or detailed. They are very useful for showing the relationships between objects, as shown in Figure 6.7. Note that this example does not show any hierarchy. To show hierarchical dependencies, you must work from the top down. Diagrams of organisations and departments are typically made this way, to show who reports to whom.

6.8   Photographs

You could use photographs to show the contents of a screen. Nowadays, using the so-called 'screen grabbers' may make this unnecessary, but it depends on the platform that the software is running on.

6.9   Dealing with the illustrations

Make sure that an illustration is not separated by a page turn from the text to which it relates. An illustration must always appear on the same double-page spread

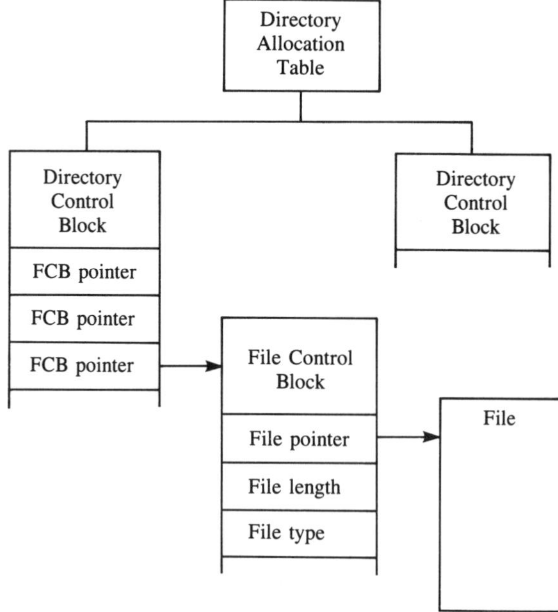

Figure 6.7

as the relevant text. If an illustration is referred to a number of times, then this rule applies only to the first reference. Where the illustrations actually appear on the page may well be determined by a standard. If not, choose between placing them in the text where they logically fit, or always placing them at the bottom of the page.

Give all your illustrations a number and a title. If there is only one illustration in your book, you must still give it a title, but it does not need a number (or the word 'figure' or 'table'). Put the number and title above the figure, unless your standards say otherwise. Number each type of illustration sequentially through the book, starting at 1. Make the titles as short and precise as possible. Follow the same rules for the titles as those for section titles.

When you refer to an illustration in the text, use only the number of the illustration and not the title, for example 'see Figure 10' or 'see Table 16'.

6.10 Summary

This chapter has shown some of the different ways in which you can illustrate your text. Illustrations can get a point across very fast, as long as they are relevant and clear. But remember that many readers skip illustrations, so you need to draw their attention to the importance of the information. Once they know that the tables and figures can quickly show them what they need, they will tend to look for more of these rather than long pieces of explanatory text.

7 Rewrite and edit

'In composing, as a general rule, run your pen through every other word you have written;
you have no idea what vigour it will give your style'

Sydney Smith, in Lady Holland's *Memoir*

This chapter covers the editor's role. You may have to be your own editor, because, even if you remember all the rules, some 'errors' may still be in the book. This chapter covers the ones that are often not found until the editing phase. It also introduces the Fog Index, which is a way of checking your text for a required reading ability level, that you can apply to your own manual. The chapter also mentions some of the PC-based grammar checkers.

7.1 The role of the editor

As an author, I have an editor. Not all software companies have editors, but, if you have one, trust him (or her). It is very easy to look on the book you are writing as your own 'pet' project. But if you do this, you will not be able to accept constructive criticism in the way that you must if you are going to continue to learn.

The relationship between an editor and an author must be a partnership. Broadly speaking, it is the author's job to describe the software accurately and clearly, and the editor's role is to apply any standards, and act as the first user of the manual. In this second role, the editor can often help the writer to rewrite parts of the book that the reader will not understand on a first reading. However well-written your book, it will never be perfect. But cooperation with an editor can always improve it.

There are some things that you can do before you turn your book over to the editor. You will (of course!) have applied all of your company's standards as far as terminology and wording goes, but there are a few typical things that you may have done which a good editor will spot immediately. These include:

- Stretched sentences
- Hidden verbs
- Redundant words and accidental repetition.

The following sections look at these items.

7.2 Stretched sentences

Stretched sentences are those that use more words than necessary to explain something which is in fact quite straightforward. They are often caused by a desire to impress, either with vocabulary, or with what I call 'companyspeak'. The result is that the meaning is quite correctly expressed, but the reader has trouble digging it out of the sentence (see Box 7.1).

Box 7.1

> *Example*
> The manual's completion date should not be affected due to the fact that it was 2 weeks ahead of schedule and that is the estimated amount of time needed to complete the requested change.
>
> *Improvement*
> The requested change will not affect the manual's completion date.

7.3 Hidden verbs

You must also make sure that you do not use 'hidden verbs'. Hidden verbs are often preceded by words such as 'gives a' or 'enables the'. They are very easy to write, because again the meaning is correct. Box 7.2 gives examples of hidden verbs, and the improvements made by removing them.

Box 7.2

> Appendix A gives a listing of the country codes.
> Appendix A lists the country codes.
> This section gives a short explanation of each message.
> This section briefly explains each message.

7.4 Redundant words

Finally, make sure that you remove any redundant words from your writing. Redundant words are those which do not add anything to the meaning or clarity of a sentence. Very often they originate from someone else's writing, such as a specification, or from the way someone explains something. It is very easy to write a sentence that makes perfect sense, but which contains redundancies that make it longer than necessary. Box 7.3 gives examples of sentences containing redundant words, followed by suggested improvements to them.

Box 7.3

> You can follow this procedure in a large number of different ways.
> You can follow this procedure in different ways.
> Humidity below 40 per cent increases the effects of static electricity, particularly in those areas where nylon carpet is used as a floor cover.
> Humidity below 40 per cent increases the effects of static electricity, particularly where nylon carpet is used.

7.5   The Fog Index

The Fog Index has been around for a long time. Originally developed by the Gunning–Mueller Writing Institute, it is designed to measure the American school grade education that your reader needs to understand your text. To apply the Fog Index to your writing, do the following:

1. Choose any 100-word segment of text.
2. Count the number of sentences in the chosen segment. If the segment ends with a sentence fragment, count that fragment as one sentence. If the segment contains a list, count each item in the list as a separate sentence.
3. Divide 100 by the number of sentences. This gives you the average sentence length.
4. Count the number of words with three or more syllables in the 100-word segment. Do not count capitalised words. Do not count words that have more than three syllables because they are in the past tense or plural forms.
5. Add the two numbers: the average sentence length, and the number of polysyllables.
6. Multiply the result by 0.4 and round it to the nearest whole number.

The result is the number of years' schooling a reader needs to understand the text. If it is too high, you need to apply some of the rules given previously, to make your book more accessible.

7.6   Using the tools available

Even when you have done all this hard work of writing, editing, and clarifying your text, some things may have slipped past you. But, if you are lucky, you have yet another tool at your disposal: the grammar checker.

If you work on a PC, you can buy several different grammar and style checkers. Some are more complex than others, but they all seem to do their job very well. You can customise some of them more than others, although this can be a time-consuming process. If you have not yet got one of these packages, go out and buy one.

I have used the first two of the following. Note that I am not paid to recommend these particular ones, and there may be others!

* RightWriter, from Que Software
* Grammatik 5, from WordPerfect Corporation
* Correct Grammar for Windows, from WordStar International Incorporated
* CorrecText, from Houghton Mifflin Company (bundled with Word for Windows)
* PowerEdit, from Oracle Corporation

If you want more information about these products, get hold of a copy of *Byte Magazine*, Volume 12, Number 10, published in May 1993.

If you are unlucky enough not to have software available to help you, then you should invest in some books on grammar and style. The Bibliography at the end of this book includes some of the ones I find useful.

7.7 Summary

This short chapter has given some advice on what to do when you think you have finished writing. As I said right at the beginning of the book, you must always read what you have written. Using the examples and tools described in this chapter, you will be able to make some improvements to your manual that may seem trivial, but which contribute just as much as all the other techniques to clear, understandable text.

8 Writing the appendices, glossary, and index

'Must the book end, as you would end it,
With testamentary appendices
And graveyard indices?'

Robert Graves, Leaving the rest unsaid

This chapter tells you what sort of information you should place in appendices.
It goes on to describe how to make a good glossary. The last section gives some
advice on making indexes (personally I do not agree with Mr Graves about the
plural of 'index', at least not for my books).

8.1 Appendices

My dictionary defines an appendix as a 'subsidiary addition to (a book)'. This
definition uses exactly the right word — 'subsidiary'. In other words, you should
put all non-essential information in appendices. However, by 'non-essential', I
do not mean that it is unnecessary, but that it is not essential for the reader's
understanding of the rest of the book. Many programming manuals include the
ASCII (American Standard Code for Information Interchange) code conversion
table as an appendix: this fits the definition perfectly.

Take another example: suppose you have to include program listings in your
book that take up more than a few lines. The reader is not going to study them
as he goes along, as they will be too long. They also break up the flow of the
text. Put them in an appendix, where your reader can study them at leisure, when
necessary.

So you should use appendices for information that does not fit in logically,
or only needs to be referenced now and then such as:

- Lists of files
- Messages and warnings
- Program listings
- Formulae
- Tables and charts not crucial to the tasks described in the manual
- Fold-out artwork
- Lengthy case studies

- Details from other publications, and other background material that may be of interest to some readers
- Lengthy dialogue examples.

You also may need to describe non-computer-related procedures that are part of the reader's work, in order to put the computer-related parts into context. It is often useful to put these into an appendix as well. For example, if you are writing a manual for a system that is used in a factory warehouse, you may need to describe some of the handling procedures, to show where the use of the computer fits into these procedures.

But make sure that the information in the appendix relates to, and is referenced from, the text in the manual. If it is not, omit it. Instead, refer the reader to other documentation where they can find this information. When you do refer the reader to an appendix, make it clear that they do not have to refer to it immediately, but that it is there for reference. You must not force your reader to turn to an appendix, and then back to the page he is studying.

Many manuals I have seen contain an appendix listing all the messages that the software may display or print. Of course, you must document messages, and an appendix is a good place for them. But that does not mean that you can necessarily ignore them in the rest of the book. Here is an example. Suppose you are describing how to log in to a system. If a user enters a wrong password, an error message is displayed. While you must include this in the appendix of error messages, you must also include it in the section about logging in. This is especially valid for tutorial manuals. The user needs to get started quickly, and requires the explanation there and then. Remember that the user must only need to turn to the appendix when something unexpected (by you and by the user) occurs.

Place the appendices at the end of the book, between the last chapter and the glossary and index. Introduce each appendix with a short overview of what it contains. By their very nature, appendices often have rather cryptic titles. If useful, put index entries in the appendix as well as the rest of the book. Do not forget to include the appendices in the Table of Contents.

You may be asked to give your appendices a different appearance from normal chapters. If not, treat them just like a chapter, as far as titles and headings are concerned, apart from the appendix title itself. This must obviously contain the word 'Appendix', while chapters may or may not start with the word 'Chapter'.

Normally, appendices are identified by letters rather than by numbers (Appendix A, Appendix B, and so on). If the pages of your book are sequentially numbered, continue the page numbering through the appendices if that is allowed. If you are using chapter-based page numbering (page 2.1, 2.2, and so on), then use the same system, replacing the chapter number with the appendix letter.

The same goes for figure and table numbering. If these are sequentially numbered throughout the book, continue this format in the appendices. If they are chapter-based, continue that format (Figure D-1, Table A-2, and so on).

8.2   Glossary

8.2.1   Introduction

Here is another dictionary definition. A glossary is a 'list and explanations of abstruse, obsolete, dialectal, or technical terms'.

The question of whether to include a glossary in your book depends on how useful it is going to be. As usual, if the reader is going to need one, you must supply one. You must almost always supply a glossary for a manual that describes new products or concepts, such as an introductory manual. You may need to put the same glossary in the training manual. On the other hand, a user manual for a widely used programming language probably will not need a glossary.

8.2.2   Choosing what to include

The best way to approach this is to read the manual again, asking yourself 'Would I (the reader) understand this word or phrase?' As you go along, make a list of all the items that you think might not be easily understood on first reading.

Once you have a complete list, rewrite it in alphabetic sequence. Then write a short, concise definition for each item. It may be that your department has a standard glossary, from which you must extract the definitions. If so, remember to supply any new terms from your glossary for inclusion in the standard one. You should consider including:

- Computer terms
- New terms
- Acronyms
- Abbreviations
- Other terms that are related to the subject of the book.

Make sure that you include any terms that you have defined in the body of the manual. The reader who wants to find a definition does not want to have to reread the book to find it.

8.2.3   Writing the definitions

If possible, you should write only one definition per word. This is often the rule in a Controlled English environment (see Chapter 10). If you must (and may) write more than one definition for each entry, make it clear when the term is a verb and when it is a noun.

Whatever method you use to do this, always start the verb definition with an infinitive. Decide which will be first, and use this sequence for every entry. My personal preference is to follow the entry with (v) for a verb, and (n) for a noun. I also like to put the verb first, as in Box 8.1.

Box 8.1

> FORMAT (v)   To prepare a disk for use
> (n)   The arrangement of data on a screen or disk

In the case where you have two definitions, number them, as in Box 8.2.

Box 8.2

> PATH (1) The route used to locate files on a fixed or flexible
> disk, consisting of a drive and directories.
> (2) The route between any two nodes on a network

Use a distinct typographical form to show which are the entries, and which are the definitions. In Box 8.2 I have used small capitals. If these are not available, use bold face, or italic. I have also indented the definitions. This is not strictly necessary for reading purposes, but it does help the reader to scan the entries quickly, and pick out the one he is interested in.

It may be that some entries must be in lower case, because the software you are describing is case-sensitive. Always capitalise the entries in the same way as they are in the body of the book. Organise them in alphabetic sequence, regardless of the capitalisation. Of course, in this case you cannot use small capitals, as I have in these examples.

For acronyms, give the expansion of the acronym first, and then the definition. Box 8.3 gives an example.

Box 8.3

> MDMS Mirror Disk Management System. The software that manages mirror disks. See MIRROR DISKS.

Most of your definitions will be factual. By this I mean that you write a concise description of the term. I call this a 'formal' definition. At other times you may want to write a definition that is a synonym. I call this an 'informal' definition. Box 8.4 shows what I mean.

Box 8.4

> Formal definition
> FOLIO A page number
> Informal definition
> KERNEL The software that controls and monitors all devices connected to the system

Use informal definitions in books that are for non-technical readers, or those that are not familiar with the subject matter. If a simple word or phrase gets the meaning across, use it. If not, use a formal definition.

Another type of definition is a cross-reference to another entry in the glossary. There are two kinds: those that point directly to another entry, and those that point to a related entry. Box 8.5 gives an example of the first type.

> DISKETTE A small, flexible magnetic disk used to store informa-
> tion
> FLEXIBLE DISK See Diskette
> FLOPPY DISK See Diskette

Box 8.5

As you can see, there is only one definition, but all the other entries the reader
may look up point to that one. The main one must be the one most often used
in the body of the manual. Box 8.6 gives an example of the second type.

> LIST BOX A box listing the files in the current directory. See also
> Dialog Box.

Box 8.6

In this way, you can refer the reader to a related subject, which may give him
some additional information, if he needs it.

In the above examples, I have used plain text for the 'see' references. You
can also use the same typographical style for these as for the entries themselves.
If you do, explain this convention at the beginning of the glossary, to make sure
that your readers understand that the reference is to another place in the glossary.

8.2.4 Checking the result

Once you have made your glossary, check it. Check that all entries that are referred
to by other entries do exist. It is very easy to write 'see XXXX', and then forget
to include the definition for XXXX itself.

8.2.5 Putting it in the right place

It is common practice to place the glossary at the end of the book, immediately
before the index, if there is one. But there are times when the reader will find
it more useful near the beginning. This is the case when you need to explain some
of the terms before using them, perhaps in a tutorial manual. For example, you
might want to explain the terms 'mouse cursor', 'clicking', 'double-clicking',
'point', 'move', and 'drag' before describing a mouse-driven interface. However,
you should only do this if the glossary is short, with short definitions. You cannot
expect your reader to read and understand a glossary of ten pages before going
on to the first chapter.

Another possibility is to include a short list of some of the terms near the
beginning, and have a complete glossary at the end. Wherever you put it, list
it in the Table of Contents, and mention it in the section about the manual structure.

Normally, the glossary is identified by the letter 'G' or 'g' rather than by a
number, like a chapter. If the pages of your book are sequentially numbered,
continue the page numbering throughout the glossary. If you are using chapter-
based page numbering (page 2.1, 2.2, and so on), then use the same system,

replacing the chapter number with the letter 'G' or the word 'Glossary'. If your book contains appendices, then it is best to use a lower-case 'g', or the word 'Glossary', to avoid confusion with Appendix G, even if there is no Appendix G.

8.3   Index

8.3.1   Introduction

The *Concise Oxford Dictionary* defines an index as 'an alphabetic list, usually at the end of a book, of names, subjects, etc., with references'. This definition, while true, does not tell you the real purpose of an index. The index is one of the most important parts of your manual, and can enhance the usability of the book enormously. A good index can:

- Provide fast access to the information
- Help the reader find what he wants, even if it is not covered by a chapter or section title
- Show what subjects are connected to others
- Give some idea of the detailed content of the manual
- Show what the book does not cover.

This means that your index must be:

- Comprehensive
- Accurate
- Easy to follow
- Useful to all types of readers.

Few writers enjoy making an index, and there is always a temptation to cut corners. But sorting the table of contents into alphabetic order is not enough (although I have seen this done). Making an index is more of an art than a science. The key to making a good index is to obey Rule 1, as usual — Put yourself in the reader's place.

There are two ways of going about making the index. You can write it as you are writing the book, or after you have finished. The next two sections look at each of these methods.

8.3.2   Indexing as you write

Depending on the tools you are using to write the manual, there are two ways of doing this. If you have a word processor with indexing capabilities, use it. If not, put the index entries as they occur to you in a separate file. The drawback to this method is that the pagination may change as you write, so you have to keep the index up to date all the time. Any last-minute changes that affect the pagination also mean that you must change the index as well.

There is a second drawback to using this method, which I have often met when editing. At first sight the index looks reasonably good. However, closer investigation shows that the ratio of index entries per page gets smaller towards the end of the book. There is a good reason for this. The writer starts with good intentions, marking text for the index as he writes. After a while, the writing is using all his brain power, and he forgets that he meant to index as he wrote. If you do use this method, you still need to check the completed index (see later in this section).

8.3.3 Indexing a finished book

Making the index after finishing the book usually gives better results than indexing as you write, for the reason stated above. A good starting point for making the index this way is the table of contents. Look for headings, individual words, and concepts. Very often the table of contents has more levels than the index will have. The conversion from one to the other is useful in finding concepts to include in the index.

Next, go through the body of the manual, in order to expand and refine the skeleton index. Keep synonyms and possible cross-references in mind.

For most manuals there is no point in trying to include every occurrence of a particular term. For example, you might want to include the entry 'Cursor movement', but you would not want to include every occurrence of the word 'cursor'.

Indexing all occurrences of a word and then removing the unwanted ones certainly results in completeness. But it takes longer, as you have to check each entry in the book itself to decide whether to keep it. In one experiment I was involved in, we indexed every word in a manual (except prepositions and articles), and then deleted the unwanted references. It took a very long time to do, but the users found the result an improvement on what they had seen before.

8.3.4 Writing the entries

You must include things in your index such as command names, acronyms, any terms that are in the glossary, essential concepts, and so on. You must also include all the relevant text from the headings in the body of the manual.

Most of the words you select for inclusion will be nouns, but do not be afraid to include verbs as well, if necessary. You can also include references to figures or tables (see Laying out the index, below). Always use the singular form of the noun, except where the entry is a generic term. For example, you may have entries under 'Compiler' as in Box 8.7.

<table>
<tr><td>

```
Compiler 21
dialog box 22   (there is only one)
errors 76   (there are several possible)
files required   27 (more than one is necessary)
installation   22
memory   23 (only one memory is used)
options   25 (there is more than one option)
```

</td><td>**Box 8.7**</td></tr>
</table>

1 Using synonyms

Sometimes the reader may not be familiar with your product terminology, and you must provide synonyms that you think he may use. For example, as with the glossary, your product may use the term 'diskette', but your reader may look up 'floppy disk'. Similarly, try to include generic terms that the reader may know. For example, if the LOCATE command is used to move the cursor, include an entry for 'LOCATE', but also for 'Cursor movement' and possibly 'Moving the cursor'.

You can never think of all the synonyms that your reader may use, of course. Look at indexes and glossaries in manuals for similar subjects. These may give you some more ideas.

2 Keeping the entries short

The main point to remember when writing the entries is that the index is meant for fast access to the information. This means that no entry should be more than a few words, preferably not more than two or three. I have once seen an index that contained complete phrases, such as 'The effect of the XXXXX parameter on YYYYY when using ZZZZZ'. This sort of thing defeats the object of the index entirely.

3 Inverting entries

Where an entry consists of two key words, make an inverted entry as well. For example, if you have an entry:

Disks, formatting 19

make another entry:

Formatting disks 19

To the best of my knowledge, there are no word processors available that will do this automatically. This means that you can only do this by hand.

4 Using subdivisions

Very often you will find that you have several entries starting with the same word. If the number of entries is more than two or three, make subdivisions. Box 8.8 gives an example.

Box 8.8

> Original entries:
> Disks, cleaning 29
> Disks, exchanging 32
> Disks, formatting 21
> Subdivided entries:

Disks
  cleaning 29
  exchanging 32
  formatting 21

Using subdivisions makes the access faster, as it is quicker to scan down the list without rereading the main entry each time.

5   Cross-referencing to related topics

Use cross-references in the index to refer to related topics. As with the glossary (see above) you can use references to a main entry, or to an entry that points to additional information. Box 8.9 gives an example of a reference to a main entry.

Diskette See Flexible disk   **Box 8.9**
Flexible disk 17
Floppy disk See Flexible disk

There is only one page reference, but all the entries the reader may look up point to that entry. The main one must point to the page that deals with the main information. Box 8.10 gives an example of a reference to additional information.

List box 45   **Box 8.10**
  (See also Dialog box)

Make sure that you do not include too many 'see' and 'see also' entries. Readers use the index for fast access. They do not want to be referred to another place in the index, and then to the page number. But there are times when it can be useful for completeness.

8.3.5   Using index generators

If you have a word processor with an index generator, use it. With some word processors, there may not be a generator as such. However, you may be able to use a sort facility to speed up the operation.

Many word processors with an indexing facility expect you to mark each entry in the text. Others can use a separate file, in which you place all the words that you want to include in your index. It is virtually impossible to create an index completely automatically the first time. However, if you have any of these facilities available, read the documentation, and use them as much as possible.

8.3.6   Laying out the index

Place the index at the end of the book. Normally, the index is identified by the letter 'I' or 'i' rather than by a number, like a chapter. If the pages of your book are sequentially numbered, continue the page numbering through the index. If you are using chapter-based page numbering (page 2.1, 2.2, and so on), then use the same system, replacing the chapter number with the letter 'I' or the word 'Index'.

Your company will probably have a standard for the index layout. Here are some guidelines on making the layout clean and accessible, in case you need to do this yourself:

- Make clear which are main and which are sub-entries. You could use bold type for the main entries, for example.
- Clearly separate the letter groups. Leave some white space between each one. Insert the start letter of the next group in a large, bold font, so that the reader can quickly locate each letter group.
- If a letter group has no entries, show this. For example, if there are no entries under 'O', put the letters 'N—O' before the 'N' group.
- If you have index entries that point to figures or tables, make this clear. Use an italic font, or a different size.
- Tell the reader what your conventions mean. Do not just explain them on the first page of the index, but repeat the information on each page as a header or footnote. Remember that the reader is not necessarily going to start on the first page of the index.

8.3.7 *Checking the index*

Once the index is complete, check it. Among other things you must:

- Check that the entries are in correct alphabetic order. It is usual to place any entries that start with a number or a symbol in a class of their own at the start. If you use a word processor to sort the index, you may find that all the words in capital letters come first. In this case you have to sort each letter group by hand.
- Check that capitalisation is consistent. Make sure that any corrections to capitalisation do not result in the entry becoming out of sequence (see the previous point).
- Make sure that every main entry (with no subdivisions) has a page number associated with it.
- Make sure that every sub-entry has a page number associated with it.
- Check that there are no cross-references to non-existent entries.
- Check that there are no 'loops' in cross-references. For example, I have seen an index that contained the following entries:
  Flexible disk See floppy disk
  Floppy disk See flexible disk
- Carry out random sampling. If you find any entries with an incorrect page number reference, regenerate the index, or check all the other entries.

8.4 Summary

This chapter has concentrated on the elements that a reader needs, other than the main contents of the book. Placing occasionally used information outside the main flow of the text, defining the terms used, and providing fast ways of finding the information are three ways of making your book readable and usable. The next stage is reviewing and testing the book, which is covered in the next chapter.

9 Testing the book

'The only test of a work of literature is that it shall please other ages than its own'
Gerald Brenan, *Thoughts in a Dry Season*

9.1 Introduction

Reviewing and testing a book is best done by several different people, for four different purposes. These are:

- To see if it correctly describes the product
- To check that the English is good and consistent
- To see that it is 'usable', that is, it matches the readers' requirements
- To see that it matches the detailed definition.

Who you can get to test your manual for each of these categories depends on your organisation. In some cases, you may have a review board consisting of 12 people, and in others you may have to do all the testing yourself. However, let us assume that you have some people available, and see how to go about getting their feedback. Note that I use the word 'review' in most of this chapter, but the same rules apply to testing.

9.2 Plan the reviews

First of all, plan the reviews. I have often seen organisations where the author delivered his manual to the software development team, only to be told that there was no time for the developer to look at it. Why not? Because the review had not been planned in the first place. Make sure that all the people you ask to look at your book know about it in good time.

9.3 Define the requirements

Second, tell your reviewers what it is you want them to review. If you want someone to check the accuracy of the book, make sure that they understand this. Tell them not to worry about anything else but the facts. On the other hand, if someone is to review your book against some standards, tell them not to worry about the accuracy of the facts.

Of course, at this stage you will have done everything possible to make sure that your book is accurate and usable, and is written according to the standards supplied. By telling your reviewers exactly what you want of them, you can convince them of your sincerity, and the fact that their contribution can help. In too many businesses, the reviewers see the job of reviewing documentation as a chore. You need to establish a cooperation with your reviewers, as you do with your editor.

9.4   Define how the comments are to be handled

You must also define in advance how the feedback you get is to be dealt with. Will you need to hold review meetings? Or will it be enough to just gather all the comments and sort them out yourself?

9.4.1   Review meetings

While review meetings can be useful in many cases, they can also be a big waste of time for some people. I have sat in a review meeting where one member of the team said nothing until we got to page 103, at which point he made a valid comment, and then left the meeting. This was because the review meeting was the standard way of working, and no-one had thought to tell him that he could just have sent a copy of the page to the author, with his comment written on it.

In addition, it is important to keep review meetings under control. Only too often, the meeting turns into an argument between two or more people, about the product, rather than about the manual. You should be, or assign, a moderator to prevent this sort of thing from happening.

However, sometimes review meetings can be useful to solve conflicting comments. But you must always remember that you are responsible for the book. Do not let your reviewers browbeat you into doing something that you feel is not right. To give you an example, I worked on a product in which there were seven different ways in which the user could select a document to work on. My team documented four of these. Almost all the reviewers, being technical people, said that we should describe all seven methods, but I resisted this, pointing out that first, the four we had described were those that the users would use most frequently, and second, that if a user 'discovered' one of the other ways, he would probably say to himself 'Hey, that is clever, I have found something that the author did not know about'.

9.4.2   Individual reviews

If you are not going to hold review meetings, then you need to make sure that the feedback is organised. The best way to do this is to send out the book with a small questionnaire, stating not only what it is you want reviewed or tested, but also including questions such as:

- Are the Table of contents and Index useful?
- Is the manual organisation correct, and does the 'signposting' work?
- Are the illustrations relevant and clear?
- Does the manual match the audience?
- Are the examples clear?
- Is the style clear and accessible?

In this way, your reviewers will not only make any detailed comments they have, but you force them to give you some overall feedback on the book. This can be very useful. If all your reviewers give you the comment 'Not enough examples', then you know that more examples are necessary. But the chances are that you will only get this sort of general comment if you ask for it in advance.

9.4.3   Giving the reviewers feedback

You also have a duty to let your reviewers know the result of their comments to you. Not only is this a duty, but it also helps to keep your reviewers on your side for the future. If you receive constructive criticism from your reviewers, tell them so. In that way, they will feel that they have made a useful contribution to your work, and will be prepared to do so again. You can do this in different ways, depending on the size of the manual, and the amount of comment you receive.

One way is to send them a revised version of the book. But there is a drawback to this method. People read most attentively the first time round: after that they tend to skim the surface of the material. After more than two revisions, they tend not to read the manual at all. After all, it is not their job to see that the manual is perfect, it is yours. Sending review copy after review copy just wears them out, and they lose interest.

Another way to let the reviewers know what you have done with their comments is to send them a short memo, listing their comments and explaining how you have dealt with them. This can just take the form of a list of pages, with a summary of the comment, and a description of the action taken, as in Box 9.1.

Box 9.1

Page	Comment	Action
19	Section heading	I agree that this is misleading. I have changed it to 'Changing your password'.
26	Section on X.400	This has been moved into Appendix B.
74	'Adding' versus 'Registering'	I disagree. While the user names are kept in a so-called register, as far as the Administrator is concerned, he is just 'Adding a user'.

Note that, in this example, I have included an illustration of where the author disagrees with the reviewer. It is important to explain why you disagree with any comment, and not just ignore it.

9.5 Summary

This chapter has shown that the methods for testing and reviewing your manual are as important as the writing. Make sure that you plan the reviews, ask for the information that you need, take all the comments into account, and give your reviewers feedback on what you are doing.

10 Online documentation

'Help'

John Lennon and Paul McCartney, *Help*

10.1 Introduction

This chapter discusses online documentation, and gives advice on what to bear in mind when creating online documentation. It also touches on subjects such as sound and motion, and hypertext, which need a book to themselves. However, the subject is too wide-ranging to be covered completely by one chapter. You should consult the Bibliography for more details of books on this subject, if necessary.

What is online documentation? You can get many different answers to this question, depending on who you ask. To some people it is help screens, to others entire manuals online. To some it is hypertext systems, and to others it is fully fledged tutorial software with sound and motion. In fact, online documentation is all the text that appears on the users' screens. The software provides the processing, and this may result in any of the forms of presentation just mentioned. For practical purposes, I have divided online documentation into four categories:

- Prompts, menus, and messages
- Guidance and help
- Online tutorials
- Complete online manuals.

You must be able to provide all these elements, but within the framework of the user's view of the system. This also breaks down into four levels:

- The larger concepts, such as the software package itself, and the relationships between its components
- The objects he is dealing with, such as files, records, items, and so on
- The tasks he wants to carry out, such as moving a file, enquiring on a name, recovering from errors, and so forth
- The syntax he must use to carry out the tasks. By syntax I do not mean just the syntax typical of programming languages and command-driven software, but also the keys that the user must press at any given moment.

90

You must also consider the audience, just as you do for paper documentation. Broadly speaking, the way you present the information for each level of user is as follows:

- Tutorials for new users
- Procedural information for middle-level users
- Immediate help for expert users.

You must design and write online documentation in the same way as you design paper manuals according to the readers' needs. This includes not only the presentation, but the style, approach, and language you use. We saw in Chapter 3 how different formats meet different needs, and the same is true here. The three types of users mentioned above need their information organised as follows:

- **New users**   New users need to learn. This means that they are concerned with basic tasks, not necessarily with the system as a whole. They need short, understandable pieces of information, and they must be able to learn actively. If possible, they should be able to test what they have learned as they go along.
- **Middle-level users**   These users need procedural information, which, by its very nature, means fairly long, connected pieces of information. They know the basics, and need to see the full picture. They are still learning some of the information, and therefore need to learn actively.
- **Expert users**   The expert users need instant help. They are only interested in one piece of information at a time, and are not concerned with its relationship to other information in the system.

Not every author is involved in online documentation, but it is after all part of the total documentation for the software concerned. As a writer, you must try to work as closely as possible with the software developer, so that the online documentation becomes an integral part of the product, and not a separate element.

Of course, to a large extent, what you can do depends on the software that controls the online part. But where you can use some recommended techniques, you should do so. The main point to remember about creating online documentation is that you must design the presentation for the screen, and forget about how the same information may look on paper. If the user will be able to print out the online documentation, then this will restrict you to some extent, unless a special utility is available for this purpose. The other thing to keep in mind is that any terms, highlighting, and so on must be the same as the paper documentation, if any.

Let's now look at some of the advantages and limitations of online documentation, starting with the advantages.

10.2   Advantages

The main advantages of online documentation (within the constraints placed on it by software) are as follows.

10.2.1 Usability

As far as PC packages are concerned, users are beginning to judge the software by the extent to which it can be used without any paper documentation at all. Games software is playing a leading role in this: I have several games on my PC which need no paper documentation, but I can still play them, and even win occasionally. But generally speaking, online documentation gives more sophisticated search possibilities than paper manuals.

10.2.2 Page and format options

Modern computer systems have many hardware and software options. It may be possible to have help windows, in which the manual can be scrolled, or searched. Using graphic terminals a choice of fonts can be made available, with bold, underline, even colour at a reasonable cost.

10.2.3 Easy editing possibilities

If the system is designed correctly, it is possible to update and change online documentation very simply, by using an on-screen editor. This also makes for fast changes when necessary.

10.2.4 Fast response times

It goes without saying that an online manual gives the user much faster access to the information he or she wants, when compared to looking it up in a paper manual. If the user can just open the book in a window, and use a search function, he is almost immediately presented with the reference information he needs. In some cases, he can interact directly with the software while the online document is displayed, perhaps in a separate window.

10.2.5 Distribution and storage

Online documentation can be distributed very simply, on disks, streamer tapes, or even by data communication. It is also much easier to store disks and tapes than large volumes of written text. And the stored version is exactly what will be used: there is no need to go through any conversion process to get it from the disk to the user, as is often the case with written documentation (albeit on disk).

10.2.6 Animation and simulation

With modern software and hardware it is possible to achieve animated manuals. This means that you can take the user through a procedure, usually using the system itself, and showing the results. This has clear advantages over paper-based instruction.

10.2.7 Training possibilities

You can also simulate what will happen when the user does something. This, is of course, a natural way to write online tutorial manuals, as the user actually does the job while learning and vice versa. Not only does the user get instant feedback on what he does, but the system can keep a record of his successes and failures. The user can choose his own pace of learning, and the software will never 'forget' where he is, or what he has done so far.

10.3 Limitations

There are, of course, limitations to online manuals, but these are few. Basically they are as follows:

- Space in the system may itself be limited, and this can cramp the style of the author. This itself can result in stilted style.
- The overall picture can get lost. Looking up something in an online manual is very useful for a great deal of the time, but cross-references and jumps must be dealt with very carefully, to keep the user completely in the picture.
- The hardware must be able to support enough functions to make the writing of online manuals worth while. If the system can present (say) only one whole screen of information at a time, in the end the user will probably just keep the manual at hand instead.
- Writing online documentation means programming as well as preparing what is to appear on the screens, and this makes it more expensive than paper documentation.
- The approach you must take to writing online documentation is not exactly the same as for paper manuals. Not every manual writer is necessarily good at writing online documentation as well.
- Some users in fact prefer paper documentation. They would rather have the manual open beside them, or be able to take it off the shelf, while they are working. This is in itself not a limitation to online documentation, but it is a point worth remembering.
- Screens are not the best medium for reading. It is more tiring to read a screen than a page of a book, and reading from screens has been shown to be 10–30 per cent slower. Furthermore, more 'page-turning' is required, as most screens hold fewer (readable) characters than a page of a book.

10.4 Recommendations

The following subsections list some recommended guidelines to be followed when writing online documentation. One can also see them as part of the design process. Any online documentation system that follows all the rules has been thought out well in advance. Where you can influence the design, in order to incorporate some or all of these guidelines, do so.

10.4.1 General principles

- Online documentation must provide the information the user needs, when he needs it. The information must be precise, and complete. However, you should still use a minimum of text: reading speed decreases by about 30 per cent compared to printed text.
- The documentation must be consistent. Consistency of user actions, displays, and wording help the user to assimilate the information, thereby reducing the amount of time he needs to consult the documentation.
- Each screen should cover one and only one subject, the one that the user has asked for.
- Where possible, menus with meaningful item names should be used, to enable the user to find what he wants without having to puzzle out how to find it.
- Where possible, match the amount and depth of information displayed to the user's level of skill with the product.
- Use headings to clearly identify each screen or window.
- Provide 'mapping' information, to enable the user to know where he is in the document, how to go backwards and forwards, and how to get out completely. This last one sounds obvious, but I have seen online help systems which never told the user how to get back to the application.
- Break the information into understandable 'chunks', just as you break information into paragraphs in paper documentation. Show how to move from one chunk to another linked one.
- Use a friendly tone (computers can appear to be like robots in old science fiction films), but do not give the computer a personality. Online help systems that display messages like 'Hi, I am your friendly helper, what can I do for you?' may be fun at first, but the attraction soon palls. More experienced users will find it annoying.
- Give lots of examples. This is much more important with online documentation, because the user wants to do something now.
- Tell the user where he is now, what he is trying to do, and how to get the result he needs.
- Allow expert users to use shortcuts through the documentation.

10.4.2 Use white space

Use lots of 'white' space, just as you would in a book. Nothing is more tiring to the eye than a screen that is jam packed with line after line of information. Users tend to think that there is more text on a screen than really is there.

10.4.3 Chunk the information

If you can use a scrolling or paging mechanism, make sure you break the information up into manageable chunks, just as you do when writing a paper book.

10.4.4   Use illustrations

If your system allows it, use illustrations. Even limited graphics can get the
message across faster than the words on a screen, in many cases. Users see
illustrations before they see the accompanying text, so an illustration can often
be 90 per cent of the information they need. However, make sure that your
illustrations show only what is necessary: cut out any details that are superfluous
to the help being supplied.

10.4.5   Highlight carefully

If you want to use inverse video, colour, different font sizes, and so on, use them
sparingly. Using a few highlights can help the user pinpoint information, but using
too many will only confuse him. Above all, be consistent: use the same attributes
to mean the same thing. Do not use more than two fonts at a time. Do not use
colour unless you are sure that all your users will have colour available.

About 10 per cent of the male population in the UK have some sort of colour
blindness, some of them having real red/green blindness, so you must not rely
on colour alone to indicate something special. Blue is a good colour for
backgrounds, but do not use it for small or thin graphic elements, as the eye has
very few light receptors for blue.

10.4.6   Match the paper documentation

Make sure that you use the same terminology as that used in the printed
documentation. For example, if the manual uses the expression 'Press a key',
then the online documentation must not say 'Use a key'.

10.4.7   Use guiding messages

Some computer software uses what is called 'Guidance mode'. In guidance mode,
the user can have a one- or two-line message displayed all the time he is working,
giving guidance on what to do next, or what value to enter in a field. If your
help system does not allow for this, you can still use guiding messages as the
first lines in each help topic. In this way, the user is most likely to get the help
he needs without having to read a lot of text.

10.4.8   Use jumps and backtracking

If your help system allows for it, make much use of jumps, pop-ups, and
backtracking. In many cases, users need help on only a small part of their current
dialogue with the software, but will also welcome the opportunity to explore,
and to call up definitions.

10.5 Summary

This chapter has touched on some of the advantages and limitations of online documentation. As mentioned at the start, the subject is too large to be dealt with in this book, but as long as you keep the main points in mind about your audience and how you reach them, you cannot go far wrong.

Appendix: Example names and addresses

'Tis pleasure, sure, to see one's name in print; A Book's a Book, altho' there's nothing in't'
Lord Byron, *English Bards and Scotch Reviewers*

This appendix provides you with some sample names, addresses, and job titles. It is laid out as two tables, as follows. Table A.1 lists twenty-five first and last names, and job titles and Table A.2 lists street names and numbers, and town names. You can use them as they are, or you can choose a different mix of names and titles from Table A.1, and addresses from Table A.2. In this way you can provide examples that are international enough for use in most English-speaking countries, and which are never the same twice.

Table A.1 Names and job titles

First name	Last name	Job title
Rick	O'Sullivan	Department Manager
Christine	Villari	Systems Analyst
Lawrence	Hall	Admin. Assistant
Peter	Lengyel	Systems Programmer
James	Siciliano	Account Manager
Karen	Clarke	Payroll Clerk
Dean	Mellace	Associate Director
Stan	Lasch	Mail Supervisor
Len	Mercier	Vice President
Cora	Watters	Programmer
Hope	Stadecker	Senior Engineer
Roy	Gutierrez	Draughtsman
Louis	Frydman	Mail clerk
Walter	Nash	Salary Administrator
Alan	Dietrich	President
Roger	Canonica	Secretary
Joanne	Reynolds	Senior Accountant
Richard	Hough	Accounts Assistant
Martin	Babbett	Support Manager
Neil	Goldstone	Sales Representative
Janis	Gaudet	Purchasing Officer
Chris	Bartlett	Records Clerk
Marty	Mercier	Payroll Supervisor
Leslie	Clinton	Support Engineer
Al	Danzig	Sales Assistant

Table A.2   Street and town names

Street and number	Town name
55 Quarry Circle Drive	Bennington
43 Elm Street	Milton
122 Federal Hill Road	Colebrook
157 Underhill Street	Sandown
147 Boston Road	Salisbury
98 Pratt Street	Alton
22 Crown Street	Whitefield
190 South Street	Milford
63 Union Square	Castleton
108 Rock Pond Road	Cambridge
90 Balmoral Drive	Wexford
33 Peppermill Road	Alstead
98 Hudson Road	Marlborough
7 Granite Street	Rochester
65 Jameston Gardens	Ackworth
21 Tenby Drive	Walford
85 Beacon Lane	Lancaster
177 Lyons Avenue	Charlestown
600 Bank Street	Beaconsfield
3 Church Road	Freemont
96 The Parade	Farmington
85 Grosvenor Road	Dagenham
41 Waterloo Way	Windsor

Bibliography

Word meaning

Concise Oxford Dictionary of Current English, Oxford: Clarendon Press
Roget's Thesaurus of English Words and Phrases, Harmondsworth: Penguin Books
The Shorter Oxford English Dictionary, Oxford: Clarendon Press

Style and punctuation

Fowler, H. *A Dictionary of Modern English Usage*, Oxford and New York: Oxford University Press

Gowers, Sir E. *The Complete Plain Words*, London: Her Majesty's Stationery Office

Kirkman, J. *Full Marks*, Luton: The Institute of Scientific and Technical Communicators Ltd

Mills, G. and Walter, J. *Technical Writing*, New York: Holt, Rinehart and Winston

Partridge, E. *Usage and Abusage*, Harmondsworth: Penguin Books in association with Hamish Hamilton

Scott, D. *Secrets of Successful Writing*, San Francisco: Reference Software International

Stephan, P. *Writing User-usable Manuals*, Flagstaff: Wredco Press

Strunk, W. and White, E. *The Elements of Style*, New York: Macmillan

Walsh, D. *A Guide for Software Documentation*, New York: Inter-ACT Corporation

Terminology

Chandor, A. *The Penguin Dictionary of Computers*, Harmondsworth: Penguin Books

Graham, J. *The Penguin Dictionary of Telecommunications*, Harmondsworth: Penguin Books

Sippl, C. *Computer Dictionary*, Indiana: Howard W. Sams

Index